GIRL FRIDAY

GIRL FRIDAY

An Extraordinarily Ordinary Working Life

Kristine Philipp

Hardie Grant

BOOKS

Girl Friday: A job title used in 1970s workplaces for a junior administration assistant or receptionist. Common synonyms include junior office chick, shit-kicker, donkey worker, general dogsbody or gofer (go for this, go for that).

Published in 2024 by Hardie Grant Books, an imprint of Hardie Grant Publishing

Hardie Grant Books (Melbourne)
Wurundjeri Country
Building 1, 658 Church Street
Richmond, Victoria 3121

Hardie Grant Books (London)
5th & 6th Floors
52–54 Southwark Street
London SE1 1UN

hardiegrant.com/books

Hardie Grant acknowledges the Traditional Owners of the Country on which we work, the Wurundjeri People of the Kulin Nation and the Gadigal People of the Eora Nation, and recognises their continuing connection to the land, waters and culture. We pay our respects to their Elders past and present.

All rights reserved. No part of this publication may be reproduced, stored in a retrieval system or transmitted in any form by any means, electronic, mechanical, photocopying, recording or otherwise, without the prior written permission of the publishers and copyright holders.

The moral rights of the author have been asserted.

Copyright text © Kristine Philipp 2024
Extract from Jeremy Rifkin's *The End of Work* (2000, Penguin Random House) on p. 202 has been reproduced with permission from Penguin Random House.

 A catalogue record for this book is available from the National Library of Australia

Girl Friday
ISBN 978 1 74379 938 3

10 9 8 7 6 5 4 3 2 1

Publisher: Emily Hart, Pam Brewster
Editor: Vanessa Lanaway
Cover designer: Regine Abos
Typeset in 12.5/18pt Adobe Garamond Pro by Cannon Typesetting
Cover images courtesy of Shutterstock.com.
Image credits: injection mold frame sattahipbeach/Shutterstock.com.
Credits from top to bottom, left to right: Ninell; Claudio Divizia; Artem Avetisyan; Elnur; Alex Pix; Twin Design; aimy27feb; koosen; Andrey Kuzmin; New Africa; Mikhail Turov; loracreative; travellight; Sirichai Puangsuwan; photastic/Shutterstock.com.

Printed in Australia by Opus Group Pty Ltd., an Accredited ISO AS/NZS 14001 Environmental Management System printer.

 The paper this book is printed on is certified against the Forest Stewardship Council® Standards. Griffin Press – a member of the Opus Group – holds FSC® chain of custody certification SCS-COC-001185. FSC® promotes environmentally responsible, socially beneficial and economically viable management of the world's forests.

This story is based on my recollection of true events. Some names are nicknames, some names have been changed, and some names are real.

This story is dedicated to working women.

Contents

1	Girl Friday	1
2	Photos with a punk	25
3	Massage and me	47
4	Bush uni admin and a housing crash	61
5	Executive assistant in psychosis	87
6	Christmas turkey hotline	109
7	That's not the deal	129
8	Unemployed comedian	157
9	Volunteering for the dole	185
10	Authoress in seventh heaven	207

Acknowledgements	229
About the author	230

CHAPTER 1

Girl Friday

It's 1975, I am fifteen and starting my first office job. I lied about my age to get the position. Gussied up in high-waist baggies, satin shirt tucked in, sequined cardigan, cork-wedge sandals stacked high, with eye shadow, mascara and lippy, I pass for sixteen.

I type like a demon on an Olivetti manual typewriter, head down bum up for three hours straight. I begin to shake my left leg under the solid wooden desk. Noon is lunchtime. I need to wee but I am already nervous about keeping the job, so I keep hitting those qwerty keys hard, returning the typewriter carriage on the ding! Just one more paragraph of this business letter, I think, my first on the job and one of thousands I will copy type over almost four decades in office work.

I keep on typing, distracted by the clock ticking into my lunch break, buttocks squeezed tight, hanging on hard like I have to at home, competing for one dunny in a household of nine.

I squeeze my legs together as the final words hit the letterhead and the carbon paper inks the blue and green bank copy sheets rolled in behind: 'Yours faithfully …' I can feel the warm wee start to seep into my undies.

The short, heavy-set old chain-smoking accounts manager looks over his horn-rimmed glasses at me. 'Time to go to lunch Kristine. Quick, or there'll be no sandwiches left across the road.' He taps the ash off a cigarette and returns to his reconciliation.

'Okay Mr Baker, nearly finished,' I say, pained face turning red.

I'm paralysed, glued to the leather wheelie office chair. Any movement will release the urine flood. I am busting. But I've left it way too late. The golden stream seeps down my trouser legs, trickling into my platform sandals. Miraculously, there is no telltale puddle beneath me.

I sit and wait till the wet dries and the office is deserted before I take a late lunch. Pretending nothing at all has happened, I walk across the office to clean myself with paper towels in the female toilets. In a cubicle I cry like a kid on the first day at school, stained but dry by the time I head home at five in my long denim coat.

It was a tough commute in peak hour in the middle of Melbourne's Antarctic winter. A tram down Bridge Road, a red rattler train from Flinders Street Station, smoking Winfield Blues, then pedalling my bicycle in the dark against bone-chiller winds, streaming icy tears, from Huntingdale Station up North Road hill.

I'm home in time to hear Mum yelling that tea's ready, then one of the kids asking what we're having, and Mum mocking back, 'Bread and duck under the table!' before a chorus echoes her stock reply. Coming back together, we sit down at the blue marbled laminate kitchen table with its faded gingham cross-stitched tablecloth.

It's Mum's payday so there is plenty of good tucker on this occasion: lamb roast with mint sauce, baked pumpkin and potatoes, peas and carrots, tinned peaches and vanilla ice-cream for dessert. One little brother (number seven), five big sisters, me (number six) and Mum chow down, elbow to elbow, gabbling and giggling in our closeness.

'Mum, I started that job today. And I only have to work one day a week,' I say.

'Which job is that, love?'

'The one at the Jag car company in Richmond – you know …'

'Good on you. Are you sure it's only one day a week?'

'Yes, they told me I'm a Girl Friday,' I say with a hint of indignation.

The whole family bursts out laughing and explains my new full-time job title to me, and my heart sinks below my asphalt-scarred knees. I only took the job because I thought I only had to work on Fridays.

A month into fourth form, year ten, Mum said I had to get a job. She had finally left Dad the year I started high school, and we went with her. I was to pay my way, with half my wages going to

Mum for board, just like all of my big sisters were already doing, and my little brother was destined to do.

There had been a couple of running-in-the-corridor incidents at Oakleigh High, so I was happy to scarper with an incomplete commercial course and some touch-typing skills under my belt. Our two-bob-snob headmistress Miss Dyer told us commercial girls that we'd all end up working behind a counter at Coles. Once I paid for fares, board, lunches, clothes, shoes and ciggies I was $10 worse off than the dole, but I didn't mind leaving school one bit. I was dreaming of an independent income, my wonderful life ahead, and a new pair of high-waist Staggers jeans like number five sister, who had three pairs she wouldn't lend me.

Since I was twelve, I'd secretly hoped to be an authoress, which is what we called women writers back in the old days. Maybe it was the hairy-beary stories we told each other at night in bed, a funny recap of our day, that made me want to be a storyteller. Or maybe it was the lack of good books in my primary school library that convinced me that I too could become a writer; all I needed was paper and a pencil. While I loved Enid Blyton and Roald Dahl stories, I couldn't relate to private-school girl adventures set in the English countryside. Their parents all seemed to be independently wealthy. The reality was, I needed to put my stories on hold and earn an independent living to afford a room of my own and bread and duck under the table. If I couldn't write the words, I would type them. So, I became a Girl Friday.

For Mum, a cafeteria and factory worker, the possibility of her six daughters progressing to a cushy office job was a huge step up. Even so, she'd complain loudly and often that, 'not one of you girls have ever done a hard day's work in your life!' before slumping into her armchair and lighting up a Viscount, pen hovering over the *Herald Sun* crossword.

Mum often told us stories about how she was pulled out of her first year of high school at thirteen by her foster mother, the old battle-axe we called Nan. Back in 1940 Nan had arranged for Mum to assist in a cake shop instead of taking up a scholarship to continue high school. There was never a time we forgot our parents' hard starts, growing up during the post-Second World War depression era. Our future had to be better than that, but their pasts were not that far behind them. Their histories held us all back.

As number six of seven it was easy to get lost up the back of the pack, and it was hard to keep up with my big sisters. I'd wait for their new clothes to become too small or worn out. Hankering for their oversized hand-me-downs, rolling up sleeves and folding cuffs to create my own style. I don't remember getting many new clothes as a kid. But I do remember being hungry and secretly searching the kitchen cupboards for food and finding cubes of chocolate in silver wrappers. I wasn't the only little kid in the family lining up for the dunny after eating those chocolate-flavoured laxatives by mistake.

When we were little, Dad would take us to catch yabbies from the side of a river somewhere, with bits of meat tied to fishing line wound around cans, which we'd usually get tangled during cast-off. One time as Dad untangled our lines from an overhanging tree branch, perched flat-out on the limb face-down, his Coke-bottle glasses slipped off his nose and plopped into the water. He cursed, and out fell his false teeth.

We wet ourselves laughing at our silly old man as he spent the rest of the afternoon knee-deep in the waterhole, sifting through the murky bottom, blindly searching for his eyes and his fangs. Magically, he found both, wiping his specs on his overalls and rinsing his plates in the creek before returning them to his mouth. Our dad was funny and lucky. We'd arrive home muddy and shivering with a bucket of nippy yabbies for tea. Mum would cook up and get us little kids, two at a time, into the bath. He was the chaos and she was the order.

When I was a nipper growing up in the late 1960s, living deep in the sprawling outer-fringe suburbs of Melbourne, middle sister (number four) was always the boss of us three little kids. We would often ride our bikes around the local university grounds, oblivious to what this manicured place was, but we knew Mum worked in a cafeteria there, somewhere. This was around the time that married women employed by the Commonwealth Public Service were no longer forced to relinquish their paid work, forfeit their superannuation rights, or conceal their relationship status.

Playing offices was one of my favourite games, saved for scorching summer holidays and wet weekends. Boss sister would round us up in the small, middle bedroom off the lounge room. We'd wheel over the sewing machine table, whip out the green manual typewriter and roll in the copy paper Mum brought home from her work. We'd answer an old, red unplugged rotary telephone, yelling reports of black gold gushers discovered in phantom countries far away, and flick frantically through shoeboxes of filing cards titled with make-believe company names in alphabetical order: AAA Oil Men and Greasy Slick Bros. Inc.

'Now take a letter, Miss Jones,' the boss would bark, pacing, and us three little kids would scramble for the pen and shorthand notebook.

As the orders and dictations got completely out of hand and the laughing, shouting and screaming climaxed, the boss would sack us all and the game was over. We'd pack up just as we heard Mum thump up the hall on the warpath.

During my adult working life, I've often felt like I'm playing offices.

In the 1920s, when Mum and Dad were born, the 'basic wage' established by the Harvester Judgement (which decreed that 42 shillings a week was a fair and reasonable wage for an unskilled labourer to support himself, his wife and three children) applied to half of the Australian workforce. Men would work and women would stay home looking after the kids, dependent and up shit creek if their husband couldn't or wouldn't work. This rule assumed that a man in paid work would gladly support his wife and children, content that women would never need or want to enter the paid workforce.

This didn't account for women's unpaid housekeeping and child care, or for widows and single women. Like the poor washerwomen taking in laundry for coin under the kitchen table, boiling up copper vats, hand-cranking sopping sheets through wringers and ironing long into the night to make ends meet. It didn't consider the stolen wages of generations of First Nations women and girls, forced into colonial servitude by the church and well-off white families.

Mum had the opposite work ethic to Dad. His was play first and work later. More like a big brother than a father, he acted as though he didn't have a large family to support. Her work ethic was drilled into us: work hard to earn your pay, head down, arse up. Her colourful verbal abuse enforced a strict order at home. Their antagonistic marriage produced seven offspring, and a fragile family life. No matter what, she was not going back to dire poverty, and she wouldn't let him drag us down with him.

Clayton was originally a market garden area with dirt roads. It was always a disadvantaged outer suburb, but it was a brand-new suburban start for Mum and Dad in the 1950s. No-one in either of their families had ever owned property before. Our mauve weatherboard house, financed by a War Service home loan, was located between our high school, which was eventually pulled down, and the deathly stench of the Huntingdale abattoirs.

There was an outside dunny next to the chook shed and playhouse, and a briquette hot-water service in the laundry with a cement trough. Nine of us fitted into that three-bedroom house before Dad and his mate Uncle Roy built the big back bedroom extension and an inside toilet and shower recess. Mum was frightened of lighting the new oil heater as it burst to life with a deep thud, spitting out wild orange-blue flames, so instead on frosty mid-winter mornings we'd play cold countries, covering the lounge room with our blanket forts, snuggled together exhaling fog like stranded European migrants.

Dad grew up in country Victoria, and had started his working life as a coal mine worker as a young teenager down Wonthaggi way. At nineteen he joined the army laundry unit and shipped out to New Britain, an island at the top of Papua New Guinea, to keep uniforms clean during the bloody Pacific War.

As the great economic depression of the early 1930s eased, Australia joined the Second World War in the early 1940s. While men were busy making war, women joined the workforce filling essential positions left vacant by men who had gone overseas to fight. Women performed duties considered to be the male domain, including farming, building and manufacturing, gaining skills beyond the home and earning wages of their own. In the postwar 1950s, populations moved towards suburban, industrialised workforces and many women returned to being housewives.

When I was born in 1960, my dad was a cleaner at the local Aspro factory, where they made headache powders for women like my mum. Later, he built dog kennels and bird aviaries from recycled wooden packing cases collected from Flinders Lane rag traders. Dad was a poor man's entrepreneur, scraping a favour from blokes he knew down the pub and reusing what he could wangle for free. He didn't read or write much, and either spoiled us kids rotten or was gone, fishing or drinking at the local RSL club.

Some sober winter mornings, Dad would make us all breakfast in bed – cornflakes and tea – in the dark before he went to work.

One morning I spied him in the kitchen, waving the teapot spout across nine cups, back and forward, then wiping up the wet mess on the table before Mum found out. Those were the good mornings.

I don't know if Dad believed in God or not, but he often said, 'Jesus-Christ all-bloody-mighty' when Mum would rouse on him for making a mess or for spending the food money. In retreat, he'd drop his caveman joke, 'Me go shed,' where we'd hide too. We didn't attend church, but Mum reckoned we could go to any Sunday school we wanted – anything to get us out of the house. 'Just be careful of the Catholics,' she'd say.

The nuns taught Mum how to be ashamed for being a poor, bastard child. When I went to the Church of England Sunday school as a five-year-old, the teacher asked us to draw a picture of Jesus in the manger.

I drew my interpretation, and the teacher held it up to the class. 'No, this is wrong,' she said.

I said, 'Shut up, you bloody bastard!'

If we wagged Sunday school to spend the plate coins on mixed lollies instead, the church man would come around to our house to collect. Us seven siblings were eventually christened Church of England in a job-lot before number one sister got married in the mid-sixties; that was the deal.

On sunny weekends, when the weedy lawn grew as high as an elephants' eye (Dad wasn't big on mowing the lawn, usually disappearing straight after Mum chucked a fit about the lawn being 'out of control' and 'tiger snakes!'), we played a game called 'mad girl eating the grass'. It was played in our backyard jungle, where we also played hidey and grizzly bear, draped in Mum's best mystery-fur coat.

'Okay, so who wants to be the mad girl eating the grass?' middle sister would ask. 'Not me!' … 'Not me!' Quick as a wink, little brother and number five sister were not 'it'. 'Come on, it's your turn Krissy,' they'd say.

I was 'it', so I'd get down on my hands and knees and munch the long grass, swaying, salivating, rearing up, darting eyes, then head burrowed deep in the wild lawn. We played the game like this: There's a mad girl eating the grass and three adults pass her by. Maybe they're kind, posh people who take the mad girl into their playhouse 'cafe' for warm lemon cordial and butternut snap biscuits. Maybe they'll adopt her and take her to their chookhouse 'mansion'. Or maybe not. Sometimes the three strangers jeered as they passed the mad girl, poking fun at her, pointing and laughing in her wake.

Sometimes the strangers were doctors and nurses from a mental hospital. They'd grab the mad girl, strap her arms tight to her body with belts and give her pretend injections with nails to sedate her. They'd carry her contorting body to Dad's cement-sheet shed, tying her down on his woodwork bench where they'd operate on her brain with his hand drill and push putty into her ears to fix her wild ways. Like our unstable home life, in this game you never knew what was going to happen next, or if anyone would stop to help.

I went to primary school with kids from every country in the world and from even bigger, poorer families than mine. Just like my big sisters, my straight fair hair was cut into a bob with a longer fringe by number one sister, a hairdresser in her early teens and a keen Beatles fan. My other big sisters all worked in offices, and my brother started in sheet metal work but soon fled to cafe shifts.

I was a short, moon-faced, meat-on-my-bones girl wearing my sister's hand-me-downs, always eyeing the next pair of jeans big sister brought home, hoping she'd soon grow out of them.

In the last weeks of grade six, with budding breasts and hips that made my pot belly look like a waist, I'd outgrown my sister's last hand-me-down grey, pleated school tunic. So, to the dismay of my elderly teacher, I was the first female student to wear my new denim jeans to primary school. I was rapt to stand out from the crowd.

From 1947, Mum birthed and cared for her seven kids, and went back to full-time work when my little brother started school. He'd been born in 1961, number seven and the only boy, lucky last after the pill became available to women in Australia. (It was initially available only to women with a prescription and a husband, and was also burdened with a 27.5 per cent 'luxury' tax.)

My big sisters reckon that's when the fights between Mum and Dad got much worse. Apparently, Dad wasn't happy that Mum wanted to return to work, and I'm sure Mum wasn't happy about it either. But he could not be trusted to support us.

Dad often spent the weekly grocery money gambling or pissing it up against the wall, coming home paralytic, or not at all. The screaming matches before school over the food money were constant. One night he was sent out to get fish and chips for the nine of us, only to return at midnight off his face. He then attempted to eat a mountain of cold flake and potato cakes by himself. We'd eaten baked beans on toast, late.

In the early sixties Dad brought home a black-and-white television set on hire purchase. Television was our escape, our free entertainment and some light relief. Laughter in our house was a release valve, masking the ever-present real-life drama. I'd do the all-elbows sharpie dance to Suzi Quatro's 'Can the Can' in the lounge room as a teenager watching *Countdown*. I remember being thirteen years old and telling my friends at lunchtime that we were all going to die after seeing the Mururoa nuclear tests on morning TV.

I particularly loved golden-era Hollywood movies on Saturday mornings, and dreamed up my escape plan, like Dorothy in *The Wizard of Oz* but without the tornado and Toto. I wanted to be Marlow Thomas in *That Girl*, with a nice boyfriend, my own groovy apartment and a good office job.

By the early 1970s, I remember screaming matches in the middle of the night. In desperation, Mum would grab the carving knife and Dad would hole up in the bathroom, leaning hard against the door as Mum stabbed at the painted off-white wood, his laughter at her fury making her even madder. The next morning we'd wake up and act like nothing had happened and go off to school and work, glad to be out of our house of horrors. The big girls started to hide the sharp knives up high in the top kitchen cupboard.

Dad was in with the local cops, so they didn't believe us when number three sister rang them one out-of-control night. Dad had lost control over himself and us, and he no longer controlled our home economics either. Drunks are unreliable and forgetful, are rarely sorry and make lousy providers. We needed him less and less and he stayed away more and more. With Mum on reliable contraception and earning her own meagre income from factory work, she could tell Dad to go and get stuffed and mean it.

In 1972, Australian trade unions and the newly elected Whitlam Labor government lobbied the Australian Conciliation and Arbitration Commission to re-evaluate their earlier decision granting equal pay to women, but only if they did exactly the same work as men. In 1973, the commission finally granted an equal minimum wage to all Australians, regardless of their sex. In 1974, the 'breadwinner' component of a male wage was removed, as more women provided for their families.

Coincidentally, in 1973, Mum finally went about packing us up and moving out. Dad would not leave his house, so we left him. We fell backwards in time to a rental dump in the next suburb, but we'd won our freedom, and home life was much more peaceful.

Dad once came to my high school drunk, asking to see me. When the teacher told me, I ran and hid in the girls' toilets, just like I'd hide in the blanket cupboard if I was home sick from school and heard him slam the back flyscreen door.

By the time I was thirteen, Mum was in the middle of a full-blown mental breakdown. We didn't notice the start of her nervous breakdown because she was always going off her nut. Still, she got on that bus and went to work at a car parts warehouse, causing her industrial deafness later in life, to put food on the table and pay the rent and bills.

Mum's factory job meant standing all day on concrete floors re-boxing and packing imported greasy metal car parts and lockwashers. Not that she could drive a car herself – she said the old man never let her learn, that was his domain. She was one of the few Australian-born women workers there. She'd laugh at her co-workers' standard reply that they didn't understand English – unless they were asked about overtime shifts and extra pay, when they understood perfectly.

Mum was invited to be the secretary of the local Australian Labor Party branch but declined. She didn't have the time, energy or ambition, preferring the solidarity and security of being an outspoken waged union member.

Weekday mornings were like a factory production line of peanut butter and sultana sandwiches and black leather lace-up school shoes, nugget-polished by the briquette hot-water service. Every school morning, she'd ask us kids, 'Have you got your lunch, your raincoat and your hanky?' counting us out the front door with, 'One potato, two potatoes, three potatoes, four, five potatoes, six potatoes, seven potatoes more.' Mum ran her big family like a well-oiled machine, then got herself off to work.

Saturday morning was housework day, starting with Mum ripping the sheets out from under you, like a magician, forcing you out of bed to help. Little brother would disappear into one of the holes he dug in the backyard, covered with a wooden fort cobbled together from timber off-cuts. Mum said it was easier for one of us girls to make my brother's bed and tidy up after him. He took full advantage of the women's housework brigade.

That is, until one day in our early teens, when middle sister, number five sister and I lodged a complaint about our brother not pulling his weight. Mum dismissed us, but we dug our heels in and went on strike, refusing to make our brother's bed. He slept in an unmade bed for a week until Mum found out. She didn't know who to be mad at, us or him, so she went mad at all of us, chased us out of the house and made his bed herself. In those days, if a neighbour visited and there was a bed unmade, it would be the ruination of a woman's good housekeeping reputation.

Mum often reminded us that 'this ain't the Brady Bunch'. She definitely was not Alice or Mrs Brady.

In our teens, on weekends, number five sister and I roared around with boys on trailbikes on unmade roads, dodging Mum's tyrannical domestic routine to ride pillion, smoke ciggies and pash on. I grew to five foot three and a half inches and stayed that height, but at fifteen – the year I left school to start work – my bosom and bum blossomed, enough to fill a bikini. We lived at the local pool in summer. Swimming until we were prunes, baking under the sun smothered in baby oil, skin turning red and fading to freckled fawn. I hid my first pimples and thick, dark eyebrows under my blonde fringe until I learnt how to pick and pluck. I threatened my first eighteen-year-old, muscle-bound, petrol-pumping boyfriend with carnal knowledge if he tried to screw me before I turned sixteen and got on the pill.

Mum threatened all six of us sisters with death if we ever came home pregnant. When I came home with a friendship ring, Mum threw it and my season's ticket to the pool into the briquette hot-water service heater. Her advice about men to us was, 'Men will stick it in a hole in the fence, so don't ever think you're special.' She was petrified her daughters would end up trapped in an unhappy marriage with too many kids to support, and no money of their own. And so were we.

At some point, word got to Mum that our old house was up for sale. There was money owing and it was in foreclosure. Mum arranged for a divorce, property settlement and secured a bank loan, unusual for a single mother back in those days. Some of us moved back into North Road, Clayton with Mum. The floors were covered with empty bottles and red bills, the vacated house was empty of life and full of bad memories. Worst of all, Dad had painted the exterior weatherboards a baby-shit brown colour.

It was depressing to have to go back there, but we were glad we had not been around to witness his decline. It wasn't our home, it was just a house, an asset for Mum, and a place for us to leave behind.

Some of us siblings met Dad again many years later, before he died. I remember his blue eyes filled with tears. He remembered me as the 'smiley one'.

'Check he's really dead, will you, love?' Mum said to us kids before we went to his funeral. At the Springvale RSL we were crudely ushered into the pokies lounge on the way to his wake in the buffet room to face cousins and uncles we hadn't seen for decades. We still don't know our Mum's pain – we felt her rage, but that was not our fault. Family abuse and neglect, alcoholism and addiction haunt relationships forever.

As a child I thought that if Mum and Dad could stay away from each other, we would all have a chance at an okay life. But like my father, as a young adult my addict self was in constant battle with my self-control. It was thrilling for me to let everything slide, just to see what would happen. As a grown woman I discovered how difficult it was to trust myself and my relationships. How often I would pick men just like my father, drunks and addicts, or just like my mother, sober, hard taskmasters.

This is a story about me, but it is also a story about women and work and persistent wage inequality.

For almost forty years after 1974, the year before I started work, a time when many women provided for their families, nothing changed. By 2012, Fair Work Australia moved to address the fact that the average income of Australian women was at least

17 per cent less than the male average, by gradually increasing the amount that people earn in female-dominated industries, like teaching and nursing.

But in 2020, according to the Australian Workplace Equality Agency report, the gender pay gap grew to 20 per cent. The gap had got wider and become more entrenched. It's no wonder businesses and governments want more women in the workforce; we get paid a lot less than men. While we may have more women in well-paid professional, leadership and executive positions these days, an inclusive sisterhood fighting for the right to equal pay for all women is yet to surface.

Gendered workforce reassignment had not shifted the gender pay gap one bit. When, to my horror, men began to occupy office jobs, formerly the exclusive domain of women, they were paid more than their female counterparts and progressed rapidly. As trade union membership and collective bargaining declined, it got worse. And as workers age, it gets worse again.

Counting on the fair-minded nature of business and government to grant women equal pay is foolhardy. It is not in their financial interests. This monetary injustice improves their bottom line. The widening gender pay gap will only be closed by determined collective resistance. We will shift women's pay inequity by regenerating the solidarity of the working class, organised and backed by trade union movements.

It is hard to believe that women's work is still not considered to be as important or as valuable as men's work. Ours is soft work and men's is hard work, so they say. Women's work and our worth are treated as less than men's. It is no wonder men are strutting around like they own the joint. The gendered pay gap is women's curse, and the cause of working-class women's ongoing social and economic disadvantage. Economic emancipation for women would move mountains towards ending macho entitlement. I hope that I can afford to live long enough to see wage equality become law. Maybe if I make it to 105.

Throughout my life, I had always felt insecure about my place in the world; not a metaphysical space, but a physical place that I could afford, a home that I could manage on my own. I did not aspire to anything higher than avoiding unemployment or homelessness. These are my two greatest fears in life, and these dual threats are what kept me going to work. In the end, they were the only reasons I had to keep a job.

Writing this story, I realised that I had spent my whole adult life working towards securing a space in this world. A warm, safe place, somewhere to write, somewhere to call my home.

As a kid watching Mum and my big sisters go off to work, I knew earning a regular wage was the best way to get myself a place. My mum told us loudly and often how much she hated her job, hated going back to work while we were still so young, and hated that the men got paid more than her even though she was the hardest worker there. But she also loved the financial certainty and not being dependent on Dad. Providing for her seven kids was her reason to keep going.

When I got the Girl Friday job it was the start of my life as a young independent woman, on my way to somewhere else. But as the novelty of work wore off and minimum office wages barely kept me afloat, like my mum, I developed a love–hate relationship with the working world. I didn't have kids to support, so what was I working for? At first it was to fund my private life, partying and going out, blowing my wages until the next payday, when I'd do it all over again. It was a work–reward cycle I got hooked on, and I was determined to have a ball after hours. Much later on, I kept working to fund my future, to have enough money to live a long life, to be able to stop working before I dropped dead, and to keep a roof over my head.

Life gets in the way of work. For working-class women, life without work is no life at all.

Women work for economic independence, to make a contribution, and to have a say about how this world is run. We work to make ourselves heard, to achieve recognition, or just to keep the wolf from the door. We work to feed kids, to care for family and to care for ourselves. Women work, and they also carry the bulk of home-based and family caring duties. I've heard working women say that they would get a lot further in their career if they had a wife at home cooking and cleaning for them.

There are limitations on what sort of roles we land, according to our gender, race and class. Too soon we are hobbled by our maturity, always by our appearance, and most often by the blokes in charge. We work as hard as and harder than men, for longer hours and for less money. We are cared for by hard-working women in childhood, in sickness, when we are disabled, and in old age. Women's work leaves little time and energy to give to ourselves, exhaustion holds us back and still we get up and go to work. We work and work and work.

Women work to create a better life and to be included as valued members of our communities. We work to help other people and to solve our own problems. We work to make change in the world. We work so we can have a choice about how we want to live, where we want to live and who we want to live with. We work to gain control over our lives.

We work to keep ourselves sane, to keep ourselves alive, and to be free from reliance on men. We work to pay off houses, to pay the rent and to make sure we are not homeless at the end of our working lives. Women work to save enough so we don't have to work forever. We work to make sure we can afford to get sick and grow old.

We stop work when we have had enough, when we can't go on, and when we are no longer wanted or needed. When our working life is done, we hope we have enough of ourselves left, and enough money to live on, to be free agents, to choose how we spend our time. We work for free, volunteering, to feel valued, to stay connected, to give back, and to meet Centrelink requirements. We retire on the unemployment line and wait to transition to the old age pension, holding back our spending and hoping we'll make it.

We work to get out of the house, to create space for ourselves and each other. To have fun, to have a laugh, and to connect. We work beside strangers and we find friends. Women work because we need to and because we want to. Without work, we are vulnerable and alone. We work because there is nothing as empowering as fine work mates, money, and a place of your own.

CHAPTER 2

Photos with a punk

By the time I was seventeen I had blown the Girl Friday job. The boss had sprung me, for the second time, reproducing anti-uranium mining pamphlets using their paper and their Gestetner printing press. I should have only printed two reams, not three – there was too much to hide, someone noticed and dobbed. I'd stashed the anti-nuclear flyers in the toilet lockers, ready to hand out at the local elections at my old primary school over the weekend. I spent a lot of time in the toilets at work.

The boss knew my loyalties to the company were fading fast when, one day, without a word, I fled the office to join an anti-nuclear march passing by on Bridge Road. I didn't want to be a receptionist, I wanted to be an activist. After two years of full-time service and consistently arriving late, I got the sack. They gave me an alarm clock radio as a parting gift.

On Saturdays, I volunteered with Friends of the Earth in Fitzroy, where I began to understand there was more to life than work and play. Unemployed, I protested more often, joining a city square sleep-in with a pack of radicals to stop the extension of the Eastern Freeway through Fitzroy.

I had moved out of home, renting a room in a Murrumbeena share house with a couple of uni students: a virginal budding lawyer (who I slept with one night out of pity), and a sweet country woman studying nursing. She was from Kyabram, where I failed miserably picking tomatoes one summer.

'Why don't you get a job up at the university, Krissy?' Mum said, months after I was sacked.

She meant in the uni cafeteria where she served surprise rissoles to struggling students and poured cups of stewed tea from giant metal teapots with two handles for kooky professors. As a Girl Friday, I also had a lot of experience pouring cups of stewed tea – as well as answering the phone, taking messages, typing, filing and smiling. I applied for several junior admin roles up at the local brick veneer university and eventually I got my foot in the door.

I landed a receptionist/admin assistant job in the Classical Studies department. I thought they taught classical music, like Bach, Beethoven and the William Tell overture. I didn't have a clue about ancient history. But it turned out to be a sweet job that led to a twenty-year career (on and off) working in offices in the higher education sector.

I figured that if I was going to do office work it may as well be at a place of learning, surrounded by books, intelligent people, and set among rolling lawns and the opportunities of campus life.

I learnt to type up exams in Ancient Greek and Latin according to a legend taped next to the keyboard on an electric golf ball typewriter. I also looked after their in-house library collection, and comforted distressed students submitting essays late.

It wasn't long before I found out that the weedy, bespectacled head of department had been exposed for infidelities with a student, which explained why he was a nervous wreck. This juicy gossip was spread faculty-wide via his pissed-off wife. Somehow, this drama only enhanced the professor's reputation as a scholarly and virile head of department. Prof managed to keep his position, no matter what rules he broke or moral high ground he transgressed. I am not sure if he kept his wife.

Yes, I liked the university sector, but it was still an office job. Once I turned eighteen (in 1978), I quit and bolted to Brisbane, like so many other young women escaping up north. Cashing in my compulsory superannuation unpreserved lump sum, worth a few grand back then, I blew it with number five sister on an extended tropical holiday.

Melbourne people say going to Queensland is like travelling back in time fifty years. Joh Bjelke-Petersen was banning street marches and public gatherings of more than three people, and the Brisbane police were notorious thugs. Against that backdrop, I gravitated to West End and joined a gang of misfits and wild drag queens. They transformed me into a fabulous punk creation with short spiky bleached hair, drag queen eye make-up, sparkly tops, stretch slacks and cha-cha heel slingbacks.

Loose on the streets at night, us punks moved in small groups while the Brisbane cops drove slowly behind us, catching us in their high beams. If there was an unlawful group of four or more, they'd try to arrest us. We'd scatter across the road, re-forming into groups of two and three, pissing ourselves laughing. We often joined anti-fascist protests in the city. We were loud and we were wild, but the cops always outnumbered us.

One day us punks were playing 'hide the slab of frozen pumpkin in the city centre of Brisbane'. We invented this game to stay on the streets in our full punk regalia, travelling in pairs to torment the police. The game involved all of us chipping in so one of us could go and buy a slab of frozen, mashed pumpkin. They'd hide it, leave us clues, and the rest of us would go looking for it. (Perhaps it was the Flo Bjelke-Petersen effect – Joh's little woman was famous for her pumpkin scones and unliberated country bumpkin persona.)

We were having great fun searching for that slab of pumpkin when my sister and I, plus our mates Daffy and Rusty, gathered on the footpath, inadvertently forming a group of four. A police car pulled up beside us.

As a distraction I did a cartwheel in front of the cops, and they arrested me. Two massive, redneck coppers manhandled me into the back of the police car, and my two mates were stunned into silence. Sitting there I remembered when our glam friend Rusty had been jumped and bashed by cowardly homophobes after a David Bowie concert. The cops were nowhere to be found.

My sister yelled, 'Our dad's a lawyer and he's going to deal with you.' The cops took no notice and locked me up overnight in the Brisbane watch house on a charge of drunk and disorderly. I was stone-cold sober and shitting myself, particularly when the cops threatened to rape me because they reckoned that I was a lesbian and their 'cocks would fix me up'.

Two First Nations women were locked up across from my cell. We talked and yelled all night at the cops, who returned to the cells again and again with vicious threats to violate us all. The two old girls told me they were glad to have a bed for the night. Homelessness was the norm for them, but change was coming. From 1970 the Victorian Aboriginal and Islander Women's Council lobbied governments on issues of specific concern to First Nations women, such as cultural preservation, land ownership and the employment of First Nations welfare workers.

In the morning I was released after paying a ten-cent fine, with no conviction recorded.

Despite the ultra-conservative government and bent cops, being in a punk gang was wonderful. The guys wore make-up, vinyl and colourful clothes, and us women wore whatever we wanted, trashy and gorgeous. With punk we smashed fashion and gender rules, rejecting our 1960s straight suburban upbringing. We reinvented ourselves to stick out and to give the finger to social norms. Regular folks would avoid us as we laughed and swaggered down the street, revelling in our wild affront and asking, 'What are you looking at!?' We got spat on and we spat right back.

I ended up sleeping with a beautiful woman friend, Vonny, a sex worker and heroin user. She had broken both her elbows falling over when we went rollerskating. She was in plaster for two months, so I helped her bathe, dress and eat. We grew close and she repaid me for my kindness the best way she knew how.

One day Vonny and I went for a day trip with our darling gay friend Peter. I thought we were just visiting friends in Fortitude Valley to smoke pot. But on the way home, Peter parked at a football field, pulled out a tablespoon, new syringes, antiseptic swabs, a belt and a tiny foil packet. Vonny asked me if I wanted a taste. For them, shooting heroin was as common as sharing a beer.

Peter carefully injected me and asked, 'How do you feel?' I couldn't speak, nothing mattered. A peace came over my body, soothed my mind, and all I could do was smile. I had found that warm place. Then I swung the car door open and projectile vomited across the grass.

From my first hit I loved heroin. But I knew it was too good to be true, or safe. I'd seen the shivers, sweats and restless aches when Vonny couldn't score or when she was hanging out for her daily dose of methadone. I didn't think about using smack again until my next move, to Sydney.

In between dole cheques, number five sister and I hung out on the heavenly beaches of North Stradbroke Island, returning to lodge our unemployment forms and party in a big Queenslander share house, camping in our mate's lounge room. We'd make our own fun stealing clothes from op shops, smoking pot, and pogoing to The Slits. But there was no work for punks in Queensland; when the money ran out it was time to go home.

I returned to Clayton to stay at Mum's and to help paint her house inside and out. But I didn't fit in there anymore.

In the early 1980s I moved north again, to the wicked city of Sydney with my lovely gay mate Jeffrey Fish. Jeffrey came to visit me in Clayton and insisted that I move to Sydney. He had a room available in his share house, a big, old two-storey terrace in Surry Hills, with some punk mates. Free from the fascist regime of Queensland, we went wild. Supplementing the dole, I worked as a freelance spectacle, selling 'photos with a punk' to gawking tourists on the streets of Kings Cross for $5 a shot. Then we'd hit the gay nightclubs to dance and con free drinks till dawn.

I returned briefly to Clayton for my modest twenty-first birthday party, featuring a rainbow sponge cake, a couple of siblings and Mum. Then I raced back to my party city, where I lasted another five years. Without checking my increasing use, I had slowly cultivated a heroin habit in my first year there, worrying my family half to death when they found out. Stupidly, I thought if they didn't see me stoned, there'd be no harm done.

Sydney is where I met my first crim boyfriend, Gaz. Gaz was a crazy punk from Brisbane who was crashing at our Surry Hills share house. He was a hard-working thief, spending time in juvenile detention from the age of fifteen, showing me his devotion by nicking a sack of red capsicums off the back of a truck so I could cook a romantic dinner. Gaz told me he had learnt to make trifle in a boys' home, but he could only prepare it for 250 people. We had a ball together at first. He was artistic and funny, but unhinged.

Gaz made a living from stealing. One night he brought home a bag of raw chops and sausages after accidentally breaking into a butcher shop located next to a chemist. Another time he came home pissed off because another crim had stolen the car he had just nicked.

He would disappear for days and reappear with stolen costume jewellery to win me over, then vanish again to work the 'night shift'. After we moved into a flat together in Kings Cross, he stole and sold my record player then told me one of his crim mates did it. Gaz had left our flat door unlocked for him.

Gaz fled north after I told him I was pregnant. Homeless and alone at twenty-two, I had an abortion at a Sydney women's health service and was offered an implant of the now-banned copper-7 IUD. It was a medical mistake and I ended up downing bottles of codeine-based cough medicine to cope with the pain. As I had an unreliable boyfriend, reproduction-wise, I needed reliable contraception. I soon got the IUD removed and went back on the pill, but continued my codeine and heroin addiction. When Gaz returned, I told him about the abortion. He was upset because, apparently, he wanted to keep it.

I went to a women's health service, told them the truth, that I was an addict, and got my tubes tied, despite the disappointment of my disappearing boyfriend. After seeing young junkie women nod off while their baby cried, I'd made up my mind not to have kids while I was in addiction. Even if I didn't have the monkey on my back forever, watching my mum struggle as a single mother was enough to put me off. I couldn't afford kids on my own, and I held out no hope of partnering with a steady guy. That would have bored me to death.

Gaz and I rented a nice Sydney house with some other addict mates, including Vonny, who had moved down to make better money and escape the crazed cops. As addict couples do, we started pooling our resources to score heroin daily. I had enough money left over from my unemployment payment to buy myself a pie and a fruit tart to eat each day. I ended up getting scurvy. I found a sympathetic doctor up the Cross who gave me vitamin shots and a lecture about healthy eating while using narcotics.

I landed paid work in an office for a community video access centre, pre-VHS and digital days. I did reception, typing, and booked the equipment. I soon learnt how to operate the chunky black-and-white video cameras that recorded onto one-inch tape. It was a good job because it was cutting-edge technology that was newly available to the community, and I met some very strange independent filmmakers.

But I found out later that my boss was importing narcotics direct from the Golden Triangle, hidden in the heels of women's shoes. There was no getting away from it. It was a heroin free-for-all, as every importer was looking for young, game punks to shift their gear. That was the beginning of the end.

I was deep in drug debt and addicted to the high-grade heroin that was flooding the streets of Kings Cross. Back then you couldn't get pot for love or money. Smack was cheap and everywhere and people were dropping like flies. If I had a choice, I'd take marijuana any day. But I wouldn't have chosen nothing, either. I kept my fantasy going à la The Velvet Underground: bohemian heroin chic, in total denial of my costly, drug-addled choices.

I mainly hung around with my women user mates, who all held down jobs to pay for their habit. Like a full-time job, drug addiction gets you up and out of bed each day, and it consumes all your time and money, too. Using dope becomes your life's purpose. My daily mission in Sydney was to go to work to earn money to score. My female mates were employed as either sex workers, office workers or community workers. We paid our way with regular income from regular jobs, unless you were a dealer.

I then started a Commonwealth public service job. My secretive double-life, public servant by day and junkie by night, was certainly not financially sustainable – I owed a lot of money to my dealer, who was working in the public service and wholeheartedly supported my job application. The job involved working as a receptionist for a departmental office in Redfern dealing with housing, construction and transport. The role was basic: repetitive typing, filing and answering the phone. I loathed the work but I loved the drugs, and as my tolerance grew, I needed more and more.

Gaz had introduced me to Mary, who became my good friend. She lined me up as the subject for an ABC TV documentary, *Faces of Change*. It was a six-part series about women and aired across Australia in 1983. I was interviewed by Anne Deveson, and a film crew followed me around for two weeks to capture parts of my life. I talked about my dreams of being a writer, about working in a boring office job in the public service, and how punks were changing gender and class stereotypes. Anne's middle-class life was as much of an eye-opener to me as mine was to her.

The program showed me transforming from an office chick, riding the train to work dressed in a neat and trim pale blue work smock, with flat hair and sans make-up, into an after-hours punk playing drums in our band Animal, Vegetable, Mineral. We recorded a song about dominance for the doco at the *Countdown* studios. It also showed me writing and illustrating my graphic novel, *Don't Follow the Leader*. This caught the eye of a publisher, who visited me later on to discuss a future book deal, but that never eventuated.

That TV appearance was a turning point. I saw how I was holding myself back, talking about killing myself by the time I turned twenty-five if things didn't work out. I did and I didn't mean it. It was used as a dramatic plot point in the program, in line with the theme of young women having no future at all. But it was based around my real fear of endless shit jobs or unemployment, addiction, homelessness and poverty.

But it was also exciting and I loved every minute. I got my thirty minutes of fame. The program exposed my creative punk working-class life and I was astounded that anyone was interested in what I had to say. I received letters from women all over Australia admiring my matter-of-fact world view. There was also one from a freaked-out Christian who warned me that I was going to hell if I didn't figure out the difference between love and lust. Later, when I found myself unemployed again, the social security officer I saw to lodge my unemployment form remembered me and told me he thought what I'd said on the show was profound.

I was even quoted in a magazine, *TV Week*, saying that I thought Girl Friday meant I only went to work on Fridays. That was the first time in my life that people had thought I was funny and cared about my thoughts. It was the confirmation I needed to propel my deep desire to become a storyteller.

By the end of 1984 our house was busted and Gaz went to jail for possession of heroin. He also copped six break-enter-steal charges and was sentenced to five years on the top and three on the bottom. His lawyer told me to get a new boyfriend. After Gaz was locked up, I dried out on codeine and pot, visiting him most weekends at Long Bay, Grafton and Silverwater jails. Two and a half years into his sentence, Gaz got drunk on homemade brew and decided it was a good idea to escape. He rang me but I refused to see him. The cops visited me at my public service office and I convinced them that I would have nothing to do with the escapee. I left the job shortly after that visit.

I had cut off my dealer and junkie connections. The ABC documentary and Mary had boosted my resolve to apply to Sydney College of the Arts. On the basis of my graphic novel, out of hundreds who missed out, I was accepted into a Visual Communication Design degree.

While studying I worked part-time as a bookkeeper for a women's housing service in a reclaimed dilapidated house in Woolloomooloo. I did accounts payable and receivable with a lovely old duck who worked part-time heading into retirement. Unfortunately, one of the housing workers was a thieving junkie and ripped off a fistful of cheques from the back of the book, putting a big dent in our tiny budget. It was low wages but I liked most of the workers there, and it felt like I was helping homeless women.

I also joined a tight-knit feminist squatter community who made cubby house nests in blocks of crumbling ancient terrace houses. They were earmarked for demolition to accommodate the extension of the four-lane harbour tunnel freeway. It was to be built to reduce travel time for busy upper-crust motorists. Eventually that freeway would push me out of the squats and out of work. I was a housing officer who became homeless.

Living in the squat, I passed the first expensive year of art college studies exploring life drawing, photography, communications and graphic design. It was a fantastic experience, learning creative skills and analysing films, media, advertising and storytelling. I felt special as a grown-up student, twenty-three years old, mixing with budding young artists straight out of high school.

But even with the part-time work and a small student allowance, the course and material fees were out of my reach. When I approached the head of the college about financial aid, he said, 'We let you in as an aggregate mature-age student and you ought to be grateful for the opportunity.' That didn't solve my money problems, so I left my studies to find full-time paid work. Still, that year of study was a lifeline. It had kept me off dope briefly, and my future started to look a lot more interesting.

During another phase of trying and failing to manage my smack habit up in Sydney, I shared a flat with my dealer. I was her roommate and best customer. It was too easy to score on credit when you lived with your dealer. I'd call Donna up and meet at her office at lunchtime, or at home after work, always scoring more and more. When my credit ran out, Donna gave my room to a new cashed-up user and I was homeless again, and deep in debt. If you want to live a long, happy life, and keep a roof over your head, always pay your drug dealer first.

My Mary came to the rescue. She was moving upstairs to a bigger bedroom and offered her old room to me, off the kitchen in the old Woolloomooloo squat. She had painted the small, damp, back bedroom sky blue, and decorated and furnished it with a pink kewpie doll on a stick, a mirrored dressing table and a single bed. It was something.

As the toilet wasn't plumbed, we had to use a bucket of water to flush. One night I placed the bucket under the shower to fill it and then went into the kitchen to start toasting some bread on an upturned baking tray that sat under the grill of a primitive gas stove. I went back to the bathroom to check the bucket and it was half-full. When I returned to check my toast, bending to the side and peering under the griller, I saw a mouse nibbling the corner crust of the bread as it was toasting. I tried to catch it but it was too quick for me. I cut the corner off the toast, buttered it and ate it.

I went back to the bathroom to find that same bloody mouse at it again, having a shower under the run-off of the overflowing bucket. I grabbed the first thing I could lay my hands on, a bottle of methylated spirits, doused it and it ran away. Mary talked me out of setting the pest on fire if I got my hands on it again, concerned for the mouse and the house. We never laughed so hard.

Heroin use ensured I ended up in shitty jobs and cheap housing in the dodgiest areas of East Sydney. One morning on my way to work, I was confronted by a pack of teen boys circling me, demanding cigarettes while they shoved their nasty hands up my dress. I pulled out the helicopter defence move, swinging both arms horizontally and spinning wildly, smashing my shoulder bag into their thick heads, then I bolted through the oncoming traffic to escape.

I had another close call when the creepy landlord let himself into my flat in the middle of the night, carefully, quietly lying on the bed next to me. I was so stoned I didn't wake up until I felt his hand on my groin. I screamed my lungs out and he fled. My flatmate, also completely out of it, didn't wake up at all. The next day I changed the locks and immediately started looking for another flat. By the time I arrived at the office, late, I was in tears. I blurted out to my bosses that I'd been sexually assaulted at home, only to be told by my laughing male manager that it was all a wonderful dream. It didn't occur to me to go to the cops, the enemy of drug users, and besides, it was my word against his. I had no witness.

Five years of heroin addiction took a toll on my sanity and my health, and I knew, like Dorothy in Oz, I had to find my way home. At first, I got stoned to forget everything. Then I got to the point where the dope didn't work anymore. Addiction had created another set of problems I couldn't forget. You can definitely die from taking too many drugs. But you can also die inside from being trapped in a job you loathe so much you need to get stoned to do it.

My last year in Sydney was the pits. Despite my resistance, social security officers pushed me into a lowly admin job at an East Sydney car auction warehouse. I paid off the last of my drug debt and rented a one-bedroom flat on my own. It had bare cement floors, it was damp and depressing, but it was mine.

At the job I penned the make, model, year, engine, chassis number, owner and buyer details into a giant green logbook. Hundreds of vehicle trades. It was my idea of a living hell. All week I sat in a corner of a cavernous warehouse full of idling motors, feeling carsick.

Each evening I'd stagger home to my little rental flat across the street, smoke pot and hash if I could get it, and abuse codeine. One night at home, I realised how sad I was and that the party was over. I decided to quit the car auction job before I dropped dead from carbon monoxide poisoning. I took the long bus ride south with undiagnosed hepatitis and a couple of garbage bags full of punk rags. I was sick, jobless and homeless, again. Worst of all, it was my own foolish fault. I was not looking forward to going back to Clayton and the unemployment line.

In Australia, when we become unemployed, we are called a dole bludger, shamed and punished with below-poverty-level support. We are forced to take any old job for any old pay because otherwise, our welfare payments will be cut off. Our colonised nation is founded on work as a type of punishment. By 1932 in Australia, back in the Great Depression era, more than 60,000 men, women and children depended on government payments called 'susso', short for 'sustenance', for food. At the time, one Queenslander said that 'many spend more on a dog' than the government spent on helping people survive. Not a lot has changed. Unemployed people continue to be blamed and denied a decent allowance to live on, especially women.

Our current Work for the Dole scheme is a punitive compulsory activity, targeted at communities with high rates of unemployment. Centrelink requires these jobless citizens to undertake fifty hours per fortnight of unpaid work-like activities to help them find a 'real job'. Capitalist ideology wants us all to believe that the market will take care of us. Work is presented as an antidote to human vulnerabilities and inequities, and as the answer to government neglect and market failures. But working hard does not make you rich.

Partnered working women are doubly disadvantaged; paid less than men and expected to take care of them and the kids too.

Unemployed single mothers struggle to make ends meet for years. When their children reach a certain age, punishing government policies withdraw family allowance support, forcing them into low-paid, part-time work while also being sole carers. Where is the financial support from the fathers?

The tired history of women being dependents is a myth, feeding class divisions and letting men off the hook. At any age, working-class women who are single and unemployed are cast as a burden on society, as poor old maids who should have solved their inherent financial disadvantage by marrying well or through blind ambition. Working women are stuck in a weird Victorian-era bind, a fantasy family model that refuses our right to be self-supporting by denying us a guarantee of fair wages and equal pay. Working women want more, and we are going to have to change this ancient narrative to get it. We are going to have to fight.

After 'mum' and 'dad', one of the first words toddlers learn to say is 'more'. Sometimes it feels like we spend the rest of our adult lives tempering our longing for more. Stuck in that perpetual cycle of desire, I had to relearn how to say 'no more'. I distracted my mind and looked after my body. I used the same willpower that kept me using dope to stop myself from doing so, but it took time.

A doctor once asked me how I got off dope and I said that one night I sat in the street crying while I nodded off, and realised how deeply unhappy I was. I knew back then that there weren't enough drugs in the world to make me happy. The stone always wore off.

It would be many years after I got clear of any niggling narcotics cravings before I could face the internal and external dangers of being addicted to dope. I would never be able to forget how out of control my life was back then.

Thirty years after I quit heroin, my past would still be held against me. When I least expected it, one of my sisters dropped a time bomb as we discussed methods of end-of-life voluntary assisted suicide. 'I'd get you to score smack for me to overdose. You still know where to get it, right?'

Every so often I re-watch the interview I did with Anne Deveson for *Faces of Change*. In some ways my twenty-one-year-old feminist punk self hasn't changed much at all. I still believe in the power of stories and that collective will and protest could change the world. But I also see that, back then, addiction and unemployment made me say, in a flippant way, that suicide was an option if things didn't improve. At sixty I changed my mind about that, after seeing too many friends die too young from despair and illness.

In 1990, sadly but to no surprise, my first lost lover Gaz overdosed after a chemist burglary. His low-life junkie 'mates' left him alone to die. My dear friend Mary rang me at work to tell me he had gone and we cried together over the phone.

Mary was a wonderful feminist filmmaker, one of the first women in her film course, and a trailblazer for Australian working-class stories using wicked humour and social realism.

Mary's last feature film, *Tender Hooks*, was based on the fun-loving but doomed relationship between Gaz and me. She gave me a book about writing memoir with an inscription saying how she can't wait to read mine.

In 2017, eighteen months after my Mary died from breast cancer, *Tender Hooks* featured as part of the Melbourne International Film Festival. I cried my heart out for Mary not being here to enjoy her long-overdue recognition. I looked into buying a ticket, but it would have cost me one hundred dollars. Instead, I stayed home and watched the DVD copy Mary gave me, revelling in our sweet and sour Sydney memories.

Anne Deveson passed away not so long after Mary. Anne remembered me fondly in her 2003 book, *Resilience*, buoying my confidence and hope for a better future that would be different to my mum's.

My resilient mum retired from her factory job when she was sixty-three, after raising seven kids and spending fifty years on the job. She was knackered and could not physically keep going to work. By the time she retired on the old-age pension, she only had the energy and funds left for crosswords and staying home.

One day, Mum confessed to me that she had wanted to be a writer too. She was an avid reader, borrowing books from the local library. She'd read in bed every night, churning through sad fictions about broken families, stories about women overcoming the odds, and histories confirming her suspicions that those odds were stacked against us. Mum was a great oral storyteller, embellishing intimate details about our cobbled together extended family. She'd drop classic one-liners describing her foster sister, who married well three times and had no children, as 'dripping in diamonds and pearls'.

But working women don't have time to write stories. We cannot afford to put our feet up until much later in life, when we're worn out from working and caring. Why is it that women's work is never done?

CHAPTER 3

Massage and me

In 1986 I moved home to start again. I knew I had run out of second chances. As I re-established myself back in Melbourne, there were even rumours of my death, but I proved these to be untrue. I worked on finishing my graphic novel while living on the dole with Mum. She was well aware of my drug habit, and she was worried and deeply disappointed, but supportive. Mum said that flooding the streets with heroin was a capitalist plot to control the workers, and I reckon she was pretty close. It wasn't all my own dumb fault.

I attended a Narcotics Anonymous meeting where they told me one vitally important thing to remember: that I would always be an addict, and that there would be no time in my life that I could afford to forget it. This also meant that I would always be an addict in the eyes of others. This indelible mark would stain me forever, long after I had stopped active addiction.

Being distrusted because of my past was the price I had to pay. Family and friends generally steered clear of me, and me of them, until I demonstrated that I could maintain a sober day-by-day existence. I also sensed a morbid fascination in some acquaintances, who would ask me what it was like going through life stoned, and how hard it was to withdraw from the drugs. I'd tell them, 'It's too good to be true, and it almost killed me.'

Around that time, I landed a part-time, short-term bookkeeper role with the Melbourne Fringe Festival, where my sister and brother worked. I helped balance festival budgets and pay cheques to artists. Some were just drunks who walked down the street the day of the parade, but if they showed up, they got a token payment. On parade day, everyone was an artist. My contribution involved creating a colouring-in book that I distributed during the street parade from an art-hole, my jazzed-up shopping jeep. It was great fun being part of the fringe arts community. It helped me re-establish myself post-addiction, work-wise, and I made some non-user friends.

By winter 1987 I was twelve months clean and unemployed. I applied for a typing job in the State Public Service Department of Health, located in the 1950s green-tiled office block Melbournians dubbed 'the green latrine', long since demolished. The job entailed typing up orders for the importation of massive quantities of opium-based drugs from Tasmania to Victorian hospitals – an eerie reminder of the proper use of narcotics.

I typed up reams of orders for medical opiates. The job was nothing but typing, I had no other duties. I used to look forward to getting up out of my chair in my typing-pool torture chamber to walk over to the magic pudding paper stack to pick up the next requisition. Like me, the other typing pool women were stupefied by the repetition. We were told to keep quiet and keep typing. There were no chats, no laughs, and few work breaks; half-hour for lunch and ten minutes morning and afternoon smoko. We didn't even know each other's names.

I used to pretend the flickering fluorescent tubes were disco lights and try to type in time with the on-off flashes, that's how bored I was. Our necks bent, our backs aching, our wrists strained, we kept typing, trapped in our roles as silent functionaries. We never complained because we were all shit-scared of losing our crappy jobs.

Repetitive strain injury, RSI, was a new thing back then and the power of suggestion gave me an exit strategy. After viewing a video about the OH&S risk of RSI for touch typists, like a battery hen with an overused cloaca, I filled in the forms to claim repetitive strain injury. I had experienced nagging wrist pain for years and now I had a name for it. After three months of churning out orders for legal narcotics, I left the job once I'd been declared medically unfit, which meant I could claim an unemployment allowance immediately. There was no compensation money for injury.

That brief stint of full-time work had helped me to save money and stay straight. But after being assessed and formally diagnosed with RSI, I took the doctor's advice and changed tack, career-wise. The doctor had asked me to think about what else I would like to do for a living. Without too much thought, I said, 'massage therapist'.

When I was a kid, we used to watch Swami Saraswati on TV, a wonderful Indian yoga teacher. I think she was my first body work influencer, apart from my mother's cure-all to 'give it a bit of a rub', and, in emergencies, a butter-ball, a lump of butter rolled in sugar. As teenagers, my older sisters and I would massage each other if any of us had a sore spot. It felt good, and I was good at it. I had also tried acupuncture a couple of times, and was fascinated by affecting energy channels.

In the 1980s, I saw alternative therapy clinics pop up as an antidote to repetitive, sedentary work. It was clear that yoga and massage would become booming businesses. I had already spent ten years working in offices and I didn't know how to earn money any other way. I really wanted to get away from a desk job, and to be my own boss. Training as a tactile therapist was a restart for my career. Even as a second job it would supplement my low full-time pay, and I would not be just an office lackey. Massage felt like more important work; giving relief to people in pain. It would also keep me fit and on track to stay sober. At twenty-six, the time was ripe for me to retrain.

I enrolled in and completed a Certificate in Tactile Therapies with fee help, thanks to number three sister. Throughout three months of intensive tactile therapies training, a friendly local woman also attending the course would swing by early and give me a ride in her van to the massage college in the city. During an arm massage lesson, in a room full of supine trainees, she raised my injecting arm and asked the teacher in full voice, 'Would massage help these scars to heal?' Apparently not – only time would do that.

Tactile therapy studies included physiology and a practical anatomy class at a nearby university science lab. I was brave enough to handle the body parts of the cadavers, which stunk like off chicken, while some of the other students threw up. Seeing a stripped-back arm with tendons – ligaments and muscles exposed, moving the elbow joint and examining the complexities of the wrist bones – was an unforgettable lesson, and reignited my passion for study.

By summer 1987, I landed my first paid massage gig at the St Kilda Sea Baths, when the venue was still full of ship rats and evening bunga-bunga sex parties. Sometimes sleazy, half-pissed male clients would fall asleep on the massage table. I'd leave them passed out mid-treatment and return to wake them when their time was up. They never twigged. I stopped massaging men altogether after a slap on my bum by a frisky male client.

One time I asked one of the old bloke masseurs to give me a rub down. I found out too late that the sweaty fella, in blue singlet and footy shorts, was an ex-wrestler. He slapped me down with slimy linseed oil then slapped me up with stinging methylated spirits, finishing off with, 'There you go love, that's it.' Highly flammable and more tense than I'd been before the treatment, I showered deeply then dived into the seawater pool to wash the cringe from my skin.

When word got out that there was a fully qualified masseuse working at the sea baths, I was inundated with female clients.

Gangs of tense Jewish women lined up for my services, telling me their life stories as I rubbed and told them to relax. I massaged a woman who'd had a stroke; cradling her limp left arm, she told me how her brain had made new pathways so she could walk again. I worked around misshapen spines and applied acupressure to the thickened backs of older women with osteoarthritis, the irreversible wear and tear of working life. I treated women who held their worries inside with foot reflexology and head and face massage, and watched their troubles melt away for a few minutes.

In between appointments, I would sit in the steam room and hydrotherapy spa, then swim in the saltwater indoor pool. I was fitter and stronger than I had ever been. It was rewarding and demanding work. I got paid $30 an hour to give a full-body treatment, while the sea baths kept $30 per appointment to make the bookings and to supply a room, oil and towels. Working eight hours a day for three months, they made a lot of money off me. I soon learnt that this was a mug's game. After becoming sick and exhausted, I left the sea baths to seek better working conditions and my own clientele.

I landed a massage gig at a women's refuge in Geelong, where number two sister was working. I would take the train down and stay overnight at her place. One day a week I would take care of the stressed-out staff, traumatised mothers and their kids, and women from every kind of broken home. Some of the women said my massage was better than any sex they'd ever had. It was difficult work, and my training in calm, dimly lit rooms surrounded by essential oils had not prepared me for it.

These women really needed someone to talk to. I got used to them talking non-stop throughout the treatment. When I could get a word in, I'd make helpful suggestions and referrals. Their lives had been stuck in high drama for a long time, they'd reached their breaking point, and everything was still up in the air. A bit of a back rub didn't seem like enough.

When I massaged their children, I could sense the years of apprehension and fear in their small bodies, and I remembered what that was like. Some would come in just to hide and play under the massage table. It was a struggle gaining the residents' trust, but over time they let me help them relax, if only for an hour. I also treated the refuge workers, who often fell asleep on the table, glad for a quiet kip in between organising court appearances, housing, welfare, newcomer intakes, and looking after their own kids.

I lasted one year massaging at the refuge then decided to practise privately from home, treating women only. Eventually, I built up a list of regular clients who came to my place for a treatment on my lounge-room floor, cushioned with blankets and covered with fresh sheets.

Occasionally I would massage a male friend of a friend by request. One appointment with a lovely gay man took a turn when he was face down and mumbled something about a stiff body part. I reassured him that I had a trick with the sheets that would cover his privates. When he rolled over, he said, 'it's my stiff neck!' not his appendage down below.

I increased bookings by offering evening and weekend appointments for working women. Soon I branched out with a mobile massage service for women in their homes. I'd hop on my bicycle, backpack loaded with an underlay, sheets and massage oil, and ride all over town, sometimes doing double bookings for couples and friends.

At one point I rented a room in a masseur's practice above a shop. A female masseuse friend was leaving for the country and told me it was available. The masseur seemed like a nice fellow, and the rent was reasonable. I offered evening and weekend appointments for women, also taking on my friend's female clients. Business was booming. Then one evening out of the blue, the masseur told me that he would like us to exchange weekly massages as part of the deal. I told him that I had a masseuse and that I didn't massage men. Pissed off, he would not take no for an answer and asked me to leave. I think he wanted my regular clients too.

Returning to mobile massage, I became fit and muscular tearing all over Melbourne, and this helped to supersede my lingering drug-user identity. I had transformed into an independent masseuse. Some people thought I was actually giving hand shandies for money. Fair call – prostitution and drug addiction often go hand in hand. But no, straight massage paid well, and it was much simpler and a lot less messy.

For fifteen years I massaged women from every walk of life, soothing the stressed out and helping the injured. It was liberating being self-employed, and I was spurred on by happy, returning customers and new referrals. I could see the relief on my clients' faces, their bodies unfurling and relaxed after a treatment. I felt satisfied and energised after giving a massage, it wasn't draining like office work. Being my own boss was exhilarating and rewarding in a way I had not experienced before.

At times I was in high demand, but it was unreliable income. Over the years, massage became a second job to supplement my office work wages. Working full-time and keeping up with treatments after hours became exhausting. As the massage profession grew more popular, insurance rates began rising and competition for clients was stiff. I also had some health and safety concerns of my own. After sustaining a lower back injury shifting heavy boxes at the office, and a few near misses riding my bicycle through hectic traffic, my small massage business came to an end.

There are so many dangers for working women. Like when massage work is confused with sex work. Or when, for example, admin roles are extended to hosting after-hours social events where a senior male colleague gets hands-on with a sly, drunken grope.

When I reported this particular incident, which occurred later in my working life, to my superiors, at first my work persona was questioned, and then I was dismissed with, 'I am sure it was all just a bit of fun.'

'Oh sorry, my mistake, but I could have sworn he had his hand high around my waist touching the side of my breast during a group photo. Silly me. But you can find someone else to do the after-hours drinkee-poos because I am out.' Faculty management wisely cancelled those events forthwith.

Women who report sexual harassment risk being branded as the office slut. That spurious label will follow a female employee forever, along with: 'You know, she slept her way to the top.'

Down the bottom of the workplace hierarchy, you've got no option but to refuse service. Women in the workplace remain on an unequal footing. It is all too close for comfort, personally and professionally, and you just never know when you're going to get touched up by some wandering dickhead who happens to cross your path. Working in university offices for twenty years, there was not one male colleague I would have been interested in sleeping with. My income was always more important to me than the company of a man.

Getting to and from work is also dangerous for women. While a bicycle offers freedom, public transport is just another added pressure. Always on the lookout for that wandering dickhead, a sleazy stare at your body parts, twisting away to stare out the window, monitoring his menacing gaze in the reflection. Fleeing up the other end of the carriage away from mumbled threats. The hand that brushes your leg as he grabs for his phone in his trouser pocket. Did I overreact or was he doing that? No, he did that.

Needled into a mindless conversation so he can try to figure out where you live. Followed off the bus by a bulge in his pants like you ought to be flattered. Walking through a park to get home, tired, alone at the end of a workday, steps echoing too close behind in the darkness, keys gripped at the ready, bolting to your front door in a cold lather. Relentless physical affronts that make wolf-whistling seem cute. How dare we walk the man-made streets on our own to try and earn a living?

It was long after we left our no-hoper father and after my massage work at the women's refuge that I came to the full realisation that financial independence was key to escaping domestic violence. Economic liberation meant women could afford to live beyond fear and poverty. They could pay for further education, get retrained and afford child care to return to work. With a regular decent income, women could reclaim economic power and secure their place in the world. Whoever holds the purse strings holds the power.

Women have given all we've got to become employable. For our safety and our sanity, women must suppress disagreeable facial expressions. If I don't smile, it means I'm not happy. 'Resting bitch face' is what I look like when I'm not on show. As my many years of experience as a receptionist taught me, it is bloody exhausting to be charming all the time. The world ought to get used to women being fully formed, independent social and political beings, expressing good, bad and indifferent feelings on our faces. Snarling for being treated as sexualised objects and fed-up with being cheap labour.

Women are calling out for the world to become more humane, and for men to self-liberate from their outdated protector-provider roles. As my Mary used to say, 'Who will protect us from the protectors?' In fact, perhaps what more women need is the chance to work for themselves.

Working for myself as a masseuse gave me independence and a necessary second income. Escaping the unrelenting demands of overbearing bosses in a stressed-out workplace was a revelation to me. Working for myself provided emotional balance, financial protection and showed me that I was capable of running the show. I also realised that I am a very hard worker and a really good boss. Unlike the average workplace, success for women in small business can be measured by the levels of satisfaction and freedom achieved, and the freedom to work with who you want, when you want.

When you're looking for work, there's a lot of talk about finding your dream job. I imagine my dream job would be in a world where I could safely get to and from work. Where I could say NO and not be bullied or sacked. Where I could make change happen from the top down. Where I could speak up without being shut down. Where bosses apologise, and remember what it's like to be a worker. My dream job would be one where I am valued and paid equally for my contribution.

At their best, workplaces can be empowering spaces for women, where professional behaviour and mutually respectful relationships are upheld and the rules are followed. The ideal workplace is one where women are treated as people, as comrades, and as equals. I dream of a working world where women belong.

But in Australia, a culture of 'mateship' – an exclusive, informal patriarchal club – dominates workplaces and ensures that women don't belong. Mateship is an implicit controlling force, a malicious undercurrent favoured by men in positions of power, who will back each other up no matter what. Throughout the lowest and highest offices across the land, mateship allows mates to get away with cruel and criminal behaviour at work. It allows them to get off on it, and to get off on getting away with it.

To challenge these mateship arrangements, women lodge formal complaints and hope to luck out on a fair hearing and decent, affordable legal counsel, only to suffer vicious trials and character assassinations. Still, we keep fighting for change, for justice and for our human rights at work. For a better deal, and for a future where men pull up their bad behaviour. For a time when women are believed, instead of being shamed and forced out of a job.

My dream job would be one where male comrades fight beside women for our rights, both at work and on the streets. Where men at work refuse patriarchal norms that belittle and degrade us all. A working world where women are treated as human beings, not as sexualised objects or whipping girls. A workplace where women are safe. I dream of a workplace and a time when men and management learn to take a NO.

CHAPTER 4

Bush uni admin and a housing crash

By summer of 1989, I'm twenty-nine and back in full-time employment as a student services admin officer at another brick-veneer university set in northern suburbs bushland.

I had fulfilled my promise to myself and continued to say no to heroin. I had got the monkey off my back, my health was restored and I needed to find an ongoing, full-time office job. One that would not be soul-destroying, maybe one that would even be career building. I also needed to secure my own housing.

But first, I needed to create a new relationship with money and work, since the novelty of blowing every pay packet on dope had long worn off. I had to find something worthwhile to work towards. I would be hitting thirty soon, so taking charge of my housing future seemed like a good way to restart my working life. It struck me that I may have another thirty years left in the workforce. Another three decades of income. Maybe I could get a mortgage like a normal person?

I wanted to become legitimate. I wanted to cover my past mistakes with a veneer of normality. Maybe joining the aspiring middle-class club of homeowners would teach me how to talk about property, renovations and interest rates at boring, drunk dinner parties. Maybe I could become a respectable and miserable homeowner, just like everyone else.

The main university admin building was a multi-level block. The second-floor offices were packed with data-entry operators banging away at bulky, red-hot terminals, creating a swampy hothouse. Air-conditioning was reserved for the giant mainframe computers that would shit themselves and shut down the whole system if they overheated. We student services chicks used to say that when we died, we wanted to come back as a computer server so we'd get an air-conditioned office.

This is where I met my dear friend Duck in 1990. She was humming and laughing around the photocopier with another work friend, trying to alleviate their boredom while churning out papers. Duck invited me to join their game; hum a song then guess the title, who sang it and in what year. We became fast friends and good mates for over thirty years. We called each other Duck and Ducky – calm on the surface and paddling like crazy underwater to stay afloat on the office rapids.

I worked for two bosses in student services; a nice one and a nasty one. The nice one encouraged me to do further study and thanked me for my output. The nasty one sprung me for posting out massage gift vouchers using uni stamps and made me pay back the $10 postage. Student services admin meant occasionally typing up heart-rending letters of condolence to the families of students who had suicided, and supporting tearful students in academic trouble. I also managed fretting academics filling in endless admin forms, who loved my work. Most of the time it was copy typing meeting notes and memos, recording marks and preparing the course handbook text on my first tiny Apple Mac computer. The rest of the time I spent at the photocopier, singing with my mates.

I had shacked up with an old Brisbane punk artist mate, Rick, renting a room in a two-bedroom hovel in North Fitzroy. When I reconnected with Rick he was half alive, curled up, crying often, battling his unresolved grief over the death many years earlier of his soulmate, Isabelle. Isabelle had died after a contraceptive implant, Depo Provera, had mixed fatally with an undiagnosed liver disease, likely hepatitis. Rick shared his neglected life with a couple of mangy cats he fed straight onto the kitchen floor. He pissed into the bathroom basin right next to the toilet. Despite his filthy personal habits, he was a great cook. In the evenings we'd eat fine Asian meals together and smoke pot, trying to have a laugh or two.

Rick had told me about a new Home Opportunity Loan Scheme, HOLS. Isabelle had applied for one of the special mortgages but, sadly, she'd died before her name came up. I didn't realise how disadvantaged I still was until I discovered that I was eligible for the low-income earner, government-backed home loan initiative. I got my name on the HOLS waiting list and thought no more about it.

At the end of 1989 my name came up for a home loan offer that sounded too good to be true. The Victorian government, in cahoots with several banks, offered me an $86,000 mortgage with reduced repayments based on my low income. I was earning around $29,000 a year for full-time admin work at the bush uni. The Ministry of Housing representatives told me I had to come up with a 10 per cent deposit, and I had to buy a house that cost less than $90,000, within ninety days. No pressure.

Back in the late 1980s mortgage interest rates had skyrocketed to 18 per cent, on the cusp of a global economic meltdown. I was oblivious to market fluctuations, and like many home-of-my-own dreamers I saved like a mad woman towards a deposit. I ought to have cottoned on to the looming world financial crisis when two months later I stood in line at the Pyramid Building Society to withdraw my $8600 savings. Irate customers were frothing at the tellers, 'Give me my money now!', and whispering to each other, 'I heard this bank is going under!' One week later, in early 1990, Pyramid collapsed under two billion dollars of debt.

By the end of summer 1990, I had purchased a quarter-acre block and moved into a small, brick veneer two-bedroom house with an outside dunny in a rough suburb near the bush uni. The house was a relic from the 1956 Melbourne Olympic Games village, acquired as public housing stock then later sold off to the private market. It had seen better days.

One morning, not long after I moved in, I spied the people across the road hosing blood off their driveway after a screaming fight the night before. It felt eerily like Clayton.

While I loved the idea of owning my own home, the reality was I had bought a dump in a shit suburb where the shops, which were miles away, didn't even sell wholemeal bread. I constantly worried about interest rates and about meeting the next mortgage payment. I wasn't on my own for long, because I had to rent out the second bedroom to make ends meet. I worked full-time at the uni and did massage after hours, and still there wasn't enough money. I waited for a feeling of housing security, but it never came. I felt trapped like a rat.

In 1991, just as Nelson Mandela was freed, I met a handsome, charming man from Ghana. Idi was seeking housing, Australian residency, a wife and children – in that order. He also hoped that I would convert to Islam. While I was keen on him, I was wary about taking on any religion for a man. And I was still reluctant to have children. But I needed someone to help me pay the mortgage, so it wasn't long before he moved in.

After two years of subtle persuasion, I committed to the five pillars, learnt prayers in Arabic and, under the guidance of another Aussie student of Islam, attempted to become a modest woman. I supported Idi's successful residency application as a de-facto wife, but a year later he surprised me by announcing our engagement at my family's Christmas lunch. Around the festive table my mother and five big sisters burst into tears. Not a good sign. They knew this wasn't my idea.

I was unsure about continuing with Idi long-term because marriage and children were not my priority. So, I insisted we go on the honeymoon before the wedding. I told my bosses I was going overseas to get married – I would have said anything to get eight weeks leave from work.

We took a wonderful trip, landing in Kuala Lumpur to visit Idi's friends from university. We hung out in the cool of marble mosques and dined on succulent biriyani and spicy nasi goreng. Then we stayed in the north of Ghana with his large, generous family.

We spent a day with the local king, who lived in a huge mud hut with a handsome piebald horse standing on straw in the front room. An entourage of the king's chiefs sat at his feet, flicking flies away with horsehair swats. The king's many beautiful wives welcomed us with freshly cooked goat stew and fufu, a ball of boiled, mashed yams for right-handed dipping.

White visitors were rare in the village. Some children ran away from me in fright, others ran behind our borrowed motorbike singing out 'Father, Father!', mistaking me for a missionary. One night Idi's elderly grandmother said she would like to travel to Australia to get new teeth and a new vagina; Idi translated through fits of laughter.

We stayed at Idi's mother's rental property – a rammed earth compound of many rooms occupied by Idi's brother and wives, his sisters, their children, and some local police officers. Idi told me his mother had made her money as a young woman harvesting salt and trading from her market stall. We were honoured with a mattress on a single bed frame, but we couldn't sleep because of the scrabbling mice inside the mattress. The air was thick with eucalyptus from gum tree forests and smoky fires, which reminded me of home.

Every morning at dawn, the women and children would walk miles to a water hole and return with full metal buckets balanced on sarong wraps on their heads, to build a fire and heat the water so that I would have warm water to wash and to do our laundry. They worked from sun-up to sundown. Taking care of everyone, that was their job.

After six weeks, we flew back to busy London and Brixton to stay with Idi's eldest sister for a week. By the time we got to Atlanta, Georgia for the Martin Luther King Day march, then on to Los Angeles for a surreal visit to Disneyland, we had decided to break up. We bought a scrabble game on Hollywood Boulevard to get through the twenty-two-hour flight home. The words that came up on the board – 'apart', 'torn' and 'no' – said it all.

Back in Australia I knew that after three years together, it was the right decision to go our own ways. Especially after Idi had bought me a whipper snipper and a 20-foot extension lead for my birthday. I also found out that he had been seeing another woman.

I did a bit of soul searching after I left Idi and Islam behind. In my brief experience I discovered that, like many religions, Islam best serves men, that religions can justify war, and that there is nothing worse than a confused convert. It occurred to me that all organised religions are highly problematic. But the best of the teachings gave comfort to so many, including me. Then I discovered pantheism – not so much a religion as a philosophy about religious beliefs. That there are many gods, and that the universe is a manifestation of god. At least this doctrine admits that religions are a creation, and that god is whoever or whatever you would like it to be. Otherwise, I cannot explain to myself who or what I am praying to when I am on my knees in deep despair, sharing my burden and sending my prayers upward to a benevolent goddess.

Marx once said that religion is the opiate of the masses. I think opium is the religion of the masses under capitalism.

In 1993, I met a fella named Will. My Mary had introduced us at a party at her place in Collingwood. I was unimpressed by his initial advances. Intellectually, he was impressive, but I could tell he was an addict. He was nine years older than me and looked much older, with thick silver hair and a wiry old frame. He dressed sharp, but I wasn't keen on being any man's young thing.

Will pestered Mary for my phone number for months. Mary told him he could only get my number if he got himself a job. Will was a printer journeyman by trade, and soon landed a good position running the presses for a company that printed one of the bush university's academic journals. One day he rang me bragging about his new job, and I invited him around to my house. We talked into the night and he stayed over.

So began our fifteen-year on-again-off-again relationship. I marvelled at the way he climbed all over the giant moving Heidelberg offset press, turning dabs of colour and black inks into pages of perfect reproduction. Will loved my graphic novel and promised to print it into a book one day.

Will was intelligent, funny and loving, but hopeless with money. He was still running addiction behaviours, borrowing money and not paying it back. Will was securely hooked on methadone, with a passion for pot and anything else that came his way.

We lived together in my shithole house for five years, and while he was happy to pay board and bills, he always owed me money. I eventually asked him to leave so I could get my finances sorted.

I was overjoyed to have my freedom back, to be devoutly non-religious, and to be no man's de-facto wife or other woman.

For seven gruelling years I struggled to keep that West Heidelberg roof over my head. Renting out the second bedroom to country and international uni students, working nine to five all week at the bush university, then treating massage clients in the evenings and on weekends. The loan repayments plus ridiculous interest rates meant I ended up with $50 a week to live on, and my credit card. The thought of two-minute noodles and fish fingers still makes me feel sick. Financially, that mortgage was as demanding as any drug addiction.

Living in an area I didn't like, and spiralling into never-ending debt with a massive thirty-year mortgage almost did my head in. This time I was doing all the right things, but I still couldn't keep up.

I came to the end of my tether when I checked my home loan statement. I had borrowed $90,000. Now, after making more than $70,000 in repayments, I owed the bank over $120,000! This did not compute.

By 1997 the world financial collapse had forced housing prices way down. I was stuck in a bricks and mortar nightmare. After seeking financial counselling at the local community health centre, I handed the keys back to the Ministry of Housing and told them, 'I can't afford to sell, and I can't afford to stay, so you figure it out.' They put the house up for sale.

One Saturday I held a garage sale and sold almost everything I owned. I kept my TV, bicycle, clothes, shoes, a plate, a cup, a knife, a fork, a spoon, and my job.

I moved into Mum's unit at a Reservoir retirement village. Not a good look at thirty-seven years of age, but at least I had somewhere to start over. I was an emotional and financial wreck, homeless and penniless. I had gone backwards, but this time it wasn't all my fault.

A few months after I left the house, I received a letter from the Ministry of Housing telling me that there was a shortfall between the sale price and the housing loan I'd signed up to. The letter said I still owed the bank over $13,000. Riding my bicycle into oncoming traffic seemed like one solution, but instead I told the bank that I was not going to declare bankruptcy as they suggested, and I was not going to pay them another cent.

The banks didn't give up on recovering the debt. The Ministry of Housing put the shortfall into the hands of a collection agency for annual visits. A nameless debt collector visited the two-room rented backyard bungalow that I'd moved into, to check that I still had no means to repay the shortfall. The collector, an average, forty-something man dressed down to his salary, would scan my assets. A foam mattress on a damp floor, a microwave in the kitchen corner and an ageing TV. He'd blush and decline a tepid drink from the tiny esky that acted as my fridge. He'd ask me the same questions and tick boxes, hating his job, and tripping over my black cat Rosie as he left.

At my lowest point, Will returned to help me with my second bungalow accommodation. Will and I camped in a granny flat in the backyard of his family home. As I completed my studies and got back on my feet, Will was a great support to me, but he was not looking after himself. I worried about him, but I needed to find my own place.

By the end of 2000, I had leased a one-bedroom flat in Northcote. When I arrived, the suburb was full of Australian, Italian and Greek working-class family homes and housing commission flats. There were a couple of old pubs and a milk bar up the High Street. By the time I left twenty years later, the High Street was full of apartment blocks, hipster bars, groovy cafes, and cushion and candle pop-up shops.

I lived around the corner from the rubbish tip, which reeked in the summertime. It had been the local quarry and produced the bricks used to build many of the houses in the area. Luckily, a few years after I moved there, the local council closed the tip and filled the giant crater to create a beautiful new park, dotted with she-oaks and metal pipes to release the stinking methane gases below.

My old brick flat was in a quiet, tree-lined street and the rent was affordable on my own. Will's family lived across the park in an old commission home. We would gather there every Friday night for dinner with his large extended family, to play cards, to catch up, to have a drink and a laugh. They were a loving and kind family, and they were relieved that I was looking out for Will.

We tried to live together again, but Will was going downhill fast. Decades of heavy smoking had caused a constant wet cough. He ran away for days to use heroin before returning home to nod off on methadone. Months later, when Will got the courage to see his GP, he was diagnosed with a serious lung infection and a vitamin B deficiency. This explained his memory lapses and his miserable cough. I insisted Will take the prescribed antibiotics and bought him super-strength vitamin B tablets that were too big to swallow. He was unreachable, and frightened.

It was unbearable to hear his chest rattle at night and then the door close at dawn as he escaped. I couldn't pretend all was well, so I sent him home to live with his family. I couldn't stand to watch him give up on life. It would be easier to drift apart, and I was happier living on my own again.

Over 30,000 Victorians were caught in the Home Opportunity Loan scam. By the late 1990s those bullshit low-income earner home loans were officially outlawed by the state government. Some borrowers had taken their lives, others remained homeless, and it had ruined all of our credit ratings. We attempted a class action but it was too expensive, and likely to fail.

In 2001, I wrote a submission to Mary Delahunty, an ABC journalist turned Labor politician and my local member. I asked her to bear witness to the tragic financial and psychological fallout from this road-to-hell mortgage scheme. I also asked her to help me acquit my debt in writing. After carrying that shortfall for five long years, the government policy and the law finally changed. I got a letter to say that I didn't owe the greedy banks any money. Christ knows what it did to my credit rating. Despite repeated requests, I never could get that information. Frankly, I don't want to know. I had got out from under their good intentions. My resilience and persistence had paid off, and I knew I would never own another home.

Attempted home ownership was the biggest financial mistake of my life. On my own, it was economically impossible to buy a house. I wish someone had mentioned that to me earlier. I reckoned the banks and the government owed me big time for sucking me into that dud housing loan that I couldn't afford and would never pay off. For sending me broke, for causing me debt, and for making me homeless.

Later I found out that a cashed-up economics lecturer from the bush uni had purchased my old house for $75,000, bulldozed it and built three new units on the block. They made a killing.

My work at the bush uni continued throughout the mid- and late-1990s, but it was all short-term contract work, all new to me. I took on various admin and finance roles in linguistics and languages, the humanities and social sciences, and health sciences. I could not land an ongoing position because they weren't advertising those prize jobs; they were promoting their favourites from within, and filling the admin gaps with the rest of us. The workforce had splintered and, as a vocal trade unionist, I was on the outer.

By 1997 I landed a three-year contract as an admin coordinator in the new continuing education unit. I produced and promoted university-wide distance education, summer courses and single-subject programs. The unit was designed to be self-funded in three years' time, flagging more big changes for the tertiary sector.

It was as far back as the early 1990s when I started to notice that many university admin job advertisements began to include 'must have a degree' as key selection criteria. I knew that somehow I needed to catch up, and fast.

By the mid-nineties ordinary working people all over the world were going belly-up financially. I was just one more little fish swimming as fast as I could, trying desperately not to get swallowed up by the debt crisis. I returned for more financial counselling, seeking some way out of the shortfall. Thankfully, a crack team of community legal eagles had banded together to push for changes to the laws governing HOLS suckers like me. A wise counsellor told me that the only way I could have the shortfall debt waived was to be on a government allowance for three years. As I was in full-time employment, I was stuck with it.

Then one weekend as I typed up a friend's thesis chapter for cash, I thought, maybe I could study at university? It would take me three years to complete a bachelor's degree. On a student allowance, I could leave the debt behind. Further study also meant I'd knock that chip off my shoulder about my underdone education, and I could continue to work. It was a simple solution to an expensive problem. A great weight lifted from my mind.

One of my managers at the bush uni noticed my potential and encouraged me to complete a business management certificate course at TAFE before applying for tertiary studies. He even granted me a half-day for study leave. I was shifting my lot in life in a new direction and it felt fantastic. The world was not going to beat me.

In 1995, as I continued to work full-time, I enrolled part-time as a mature-age student in a Bachelor of Arts degree majoring in media and cinema studies. I was rapt to be studying two of my favourite things, film and TV. I signed up for classical Hollywood cinema and Australian television subjects, and a media production program. Fancy going to university to watch films and TV shows! I was in screen heaven, and hungry for a decent education.

Keen as mustard to attend my first cinema studies lecture, I entered a giant, tiered theatre and sat in the middle row to get a good view of the miniature lecturer standing in front of a projection screen and behind a lectern. He welcomed us to our study journey then started talking about volcanos, showing slides of Krakatoa and exploding molten lava. I assumed he was referencing the genre of disaster films. I noticed a number of confused students' faces next to me. He then announced that anyone who was not there for Earth Sciences was in the wrong lecture theatre and should move to the one next door. About thirty of us starry-eyed movie buffs got up and left.

Walking into the massive university library as a first-year undergraduate student was overwhelming. Dizzy with possibilities, thousands of books were waiting, and the Dewey decimal system beckoned. It was like I had come home to a place I never really knew I had missed.

My whole focus shifted from dramas at work to dramas on the screen, reading film theory and studying great comic Hollywood directors like Billy Wilder, and precocious innovators like Orson Welles. We analysed the opening sequence of *The Simpsons*, noting how they were all coming home to watch television, a self-reflexive device of popular culture.

I studied the politics of taste, and analysed gaslight melodramas full of menace and discontent. We watched classic Hollywood heartbreakers like *Rebel Without a Cause*, and some truly revolting French film by a weirdo director who thought shit being flung at a woman tied to a tree was of artistic merit. We examined in close-up what the phallic walking stick with a pop-out knife blade really meant in *Gilda* with gorgeous Rita Hayworth. We took a deep dive into Marxist-feminist film theory. We critiqued the news and current affairs, and made a short video for a group assignment about big-mouthed women. At lunchtime seminars I learnt how to think critically, how to frame an academic argument and how to write an essay. I expanded my intellect and unlearnt a whole lot of stuff I thought I knew for sure. I thirsted for more.

In the second year of study, I went full-time and was granted a student allowance so I could work part-time. I was excelling with high marks and loving every minute of it. I was also awarded a fee scholarship worth thousands of dollars. I even went on to complete an honours year thesis, supported by an equity and merit grant. At last, I was being rewarded for being smart and poor. The younger students would say that I only got good marks and a scholarship because I didn't have a life. I told them I had a life once, and it was incredible.

At my graduation ceremony in 2000, my mum jumped to her feet to give me a solo standing ovation, while my brother and my study champion Will both beamed with pride. I waved my degree tube as I strode past my smiling employers, doffing my cap as they gave a nod to my belated academic success. There I was, an old Girl Friday from Clayton who had made good.

Further study was not only my ticket to continuing employment in university offices, it also recast me as a better-late-than-never success story. They were some of the best years of my life, working and studying. A copy of my honours thesis, *TV chat shows: Sites of resistance or conformity?* was also placed on one of those scary university library shelves.

Heading towards forty, I was old enough to appreciate the transformative power of a good education. With the sheer volume of graduates being produced, the most basic admin jobs that I'd once waltzed into now required a degree. The university sector was also shifting away from degrees for academia towards degrees designed for professions, to help students get into the workforce, which would also help pay back fee debts. A university degree meant employability. And employment transforms lives. I would have loved to work in the media sector, but as our lecturer mentioned at our last class, 'You need to be related to or very close to someone in the media to get your foot in the door.'

One of the lowlights of my ten years working and studying at the bush uni was when I returned from leave to find my job had been filled by someone else. My two bosses had recruited a younger, more compliant woman. I was shunted to the university's research office, to file and hand out grant application forms to academics. This was the early computer days, when paperwork still ruled.

One day, Professor Pompous came to pick up a research grant form. New to the role, I didn't realise that the form I'd handed him was out of date. That afternoon he returned to my hallway desk to bawl me out.

'You've given me last year's form. Don't you know what you're doing? How many others have missed out on a research grant because of your incompetence?' he bellowed.

I apologised and quickly arranged for the current forms to be posted. I then overhauled and updated the neglected paper-based research filing system. I rang Prof Pompous to ask him to collect the current grant application. He arrived with a research fellow in tow, and was still blabbing on about the wrong forms. I was stony faced as I handed him the papers.

'Here you go,' I said, then busted out a fake smile.

'Are you the most obnoxious person in this office?' he said, snatching the forms.

'Yes,' I said, 'I am.'

While working in the continuing education coordinator role, the bush uni put a penny-pinching finance manager in charge of overseeing budget reductions. This included getting the maintenance guys to saw university-issued soap bars in half so the students would stop stealing them from the toilets.

The budget slash and burn had the university's wildlife reserves in their sights. Located at the back of the campus, the reserves provided a vital wildlife corridor of wetlands and woodlands. It was beautiful conserved bushland used for environmental studies, research projects, education and as a breathing space. These nature reserves were on campus land, and provided a buffer for the surrounding areas of light industrial and suburban sprawl.

I had started working with my lefty mate Jorge, promoting twilight tours of the nature reserves to the general public in the continuing education programs. We became fast eco-friendly friends. Our professional partnership bloomed as we cooked up a plan to save the university's wildlife reserves from being merged into the campus grounds budget, to be cut in half like soap bars or developed out of existence. Jorge and I produced a wildlife reserves triannual report, the first one ever. The report highlighted the long history of the area, and the work of the wonderful staff and volunteers who helped to preserve the bushland for populations of birds, fish, frogs, possums, bats, reptiles, kangaroos and humans.

We released the report and arranged a private full moon tour and bush barbecue under the ironbark trees in the wildlife reserves. We invited the Vice-Chancellor, his wife and a VIP friend to show the big boss what it was all about. The V-C told us he had never visited the reserves before, and he was impressed by our report and the beauty of the wetland sanctuary and forest at dusk. As the full moon lit the starry sky, shadows of eastern grey kangaroos watched us cook gourmet snags over a crackling fire, served with plenty of decent red wine. We slowly convinced the V-C to protect this precious wild patch.

Jorge and I and the volunteers saved the wildlife reserves, and they're still going stronger than ever, with an indigenous plant nursery and regular public events. As an office worker you rarely get to make a lasting contribution to the wider world. This was mine.

After I graduated in 2000, I landed my last one-year contract office gig in the school of philosophy. After ten years of working at the bush uni, I applied for long service leave. Overnight, the HR rules had changed, allowing only a three-day break between contracts. I'd had a four-day break between jobs. I lost three months of paid long service leave, and the bush university met their budget targets.

In 2001 I got a full-time job as an admin coordinator supporting a new cross-discipline creative program at a Melbourne arts college. They taught filmmaking, acting, dance, music, theatre, visual design and fine arts. I really wanted to study there but I couldn't afford it, so the next best thing was to work there.

For two years I assisted with the rollout of a collaborative curriculum, hosting fabulously obscure international guest speakers, including a masked revolutionary from the Sandinistas. The cross-disciplinary program encouraged musicians to dance, theatre makers to paint, and filmmakers to act. The driven arts students were cajoled into unfamiliar practices as a compulsory part of their course.

Meanwhile, I lugged bulky TV sets across campus to portable classrooms, got patted on the head by one boss, literally, and generally ran around like a blue-arse fly. Staff were expected to be married to their job. It was all lovey-dovey artsy-fartsy, but I wasn't up for the twelve-hour working days.

One lunchtime at the college cafe, the director swanned by to tell me she wanted me to contact Nina Simone, the black civil rights activist, singer, composer, superstar legend, and graduate of the Juilliard School of Music. 'Tell Nina that the college has decided to award her an honorary degree,' she declared.

'I'm not sure Ms Simone would be willing to fly all the way to Melbourne from the USA for such an honour, but I'll check,' I replied.

It was a direct order from the big boss, so I went about finding a way to contact Nina Simone's agent. I discovered she had already received multiple honorariums, and that she did not like to fly. I also found her agent's email and wrote a polite, optional email inviting Ms Simone to an end-of-year graduation ceremony to receive her honorary award from our dinky little down-under arts college. The next day the 9/11 attack hit America's twin towers, and that was the end of that.

The academic boss was a good fella, a fine boss and a good-looker, with a strong nose and shoulder-length curls. One afternoon, he returned to the office disturbed. He confided in me that the ageing college director had grabbed his knee and promised to make him a professor. Madame Director was a tall drink of a woman who looked down her nose at everyone. Her unwanted advances had shaken him. Sexual harassment was one thing, but to add insult to injury, Madame Director didn't understand the strict rules of academic promotion. Handsome boss abruptly left the job and fled to pursue a successful academic career elsewhere.

Admin boss, the Terrier, appointed a junior lecturer to manage the college-wide teaching program and guest lecture series. The junior lecturer was into dropping ecstasy tabs, often, and was soon up the duff after a liaison with a visiting guest artist, and well on her way to maternity leave.

In a tizz, the Terrier insisted I manage the centre on my own, with no academic leadership, telling me that everything would be fine. As I watched the program fall apart and after copping earfuls from the staff, students and guest artists, I made my plans to get another job. As the semester ended, I gave the admin boss my notice, having received a job offer from a university up the road.

'But you can't leave, I won't let you,' said the Terrier.
'But I have no more left to give.'

After I bought that godforsaken house I was supposed to feel secure. I was supposed to feel like I had achieved something big. All I remember is a year-long headache, a rising sense of dread, and debt that would follow me to my grave. At my lowest point, I threw myself on the threadbare, nylon carpet of my barely furnished lounge room and wailed.

Unemployment and homelessness made me feel desperate and alone. I became unhitched, my life spun in reverse. I was adrift in a hostile world, I had lost my place in it, and it was difficult to regain purchase. Work equals housing and housing means work. When your working life goes tits-up, keeping your housing is hard work. When your housing goes tits-up, it is impossible to keep a job.

Back in the 1960s and 1970s, 'the personal is political' was the rallying cry of working-class feminists. The phrase came out of the mouths of millions of women in public and private conversations, at work and at home. Back then, women objected to the politicisation of women's reproductive rights, rejected the nuclear family model, and challenged the idea of the subservient wife and mother. In 1961, women's lib got real when women were given access to the contraceptive pill. Men were no longer in birth control of their wives. This changed the dynamics of families forever.

By the 1980s, during an era of strong trade union membership, we stood up for the rights of women, calling out sexism and racism in the workplace. Unionists also stopped developers gentrifying working-class suburbs with green bans, and halted destructive mining companies. Back in the olden days, worker solidarity saw women and men stand together to fight for better conditions, fair wages, and for safe and secure work. It was a golden time when workers went on strike for personal, political, environmental and social change.

Then in the 1990s, the global financial crisis was the epitome of the personal being political as households spiralled into unemployment, poverty and homelessness. I was just one of them. It was only after I attended a lecture at the arts college where I had worked, and listened to a guest speaker describe the real-world impacts of economic collapses, that I understood the broader context of my housing downfall. I learnt a 'personal is political' lesson I would never forget: when the world is in a fiscal feeding frenzy, governments and banks are predators, and low-income people are their prey. And the banks can't lose.

For women, a home is so much more than a roof to keep the rain off. Housing gives us a private sanctuary and a home base. My work provided me with a place to live, a space to feel human. But it can be taken away in the blink of an eye. As Dorothy in Oz repeats as she clicks her ruby heels together, 'there's no place like home', even as she returns to her twister-ravaged, dustbowl farm.

In my early forties, I faced the fact that I would be working for many more years to come, so I figured I'd better get my act together. A secure job was my necessity, it gave me a living wage, bread and duck under the table, and a roof over my head. Work is my freedom from homelessness and poverty. But no working-class woman can be sure about her financial future, ever.

CHAPTER 5

Executive assistant in psychosis

I HAD NEVER LIKED the monotony and grinding regularity of admin work. Who does? Nothing exciting ever resulted from all those pages of minutes taken in all those endless meetings. No laughs, no fun. I was always on the run for everyone. I was the back-end support person, a well-dressed process worker, a white-collar wage-slave at everyone's beck and call. I was surrounded by the successful and well-heeled, but I was in their service and had no connection to their world. Although I did meet Dame Elisabeth Murdoch once, at an event hosted by the arts college. She had very big hands, but they offered nothing to me.

In early 2002, aged forty-two, I took a step up as an executive assistant to the dean of a faculty at a university. First, I was to oversee the packing up and moving on of the old dean, Professor Sad, a dictatorial white-haired academic forced to relinquish his position with a handsome early retirement package. After years of hard-arsed leadership, everyone was glad to see the back of him. He didn't want to leave, and promptly took a month's absence while I boxed up his ten years of research papers and shelves full of books.

The new dean, Professor Bea, was a wonderful boss, a humanist and the first woman to take up the coveted academic post. She was a joy to work with and we covertly raised the feminist fist to the established pale, male and stale order.

As the dean's door bitch, part of my job was to turn away academics expecting promotion, failing students begging for a second chance, and duelling scholars fighting over building renovations. I quickly discovered that ego stroking and breaking up fights was part of the job.

One senior professor, a rotund, bow-tied, balding historian, was a sore loser who saw himself as the obvious successor to Professor Sad. Senior Prof was institutionalised cradle to the grave – his father had been dean many moons ago, and had designed the faculty building we occupied, which was later discovered to be filled with asbestos. During office renovations, we removed a large oil painting of his old man; his dead eyes followed you around the room. Prof Bea asked me to relocate the haunted portrait – I left it outside Senior Prof's office.

My new role began with sorting and boxing hundreds of yellowing manila folders, fading archives bound for the tip in seven years' time. I spotted a bulging file, an old compensation claim. Years ago, Senior Prof had invited a group of post-graduates to his home after their ceremony. During celebrations, he cracked open a bottle of bubbly and popped the cork into his eye socket. For three years he chased money for his pain and suffering. The compo committee found that during his after-hours actions he had suffered a self-inflicted injury. He got nothing. That fat file made my day.

I also discovered that, one semester, he gave every student in his course with a Chinese family name a fail grade of 49 per cent. I had collated these student results for the dean to sign off and pointed out the odd consistency. Prof Bea pulled Senior Prof up in academic progress committee and told him to re-mark the students' work; he gave them all the same 50 per cent pass mark. Rumour had it that Senior Prof was at an old boys' lunch at the staff club soon after and called out the new dean for favouring the Chinese students.

When word got back to Prof Bea she was rattled. I told her, 'Dob him in for academic misconduct, call out his racism, and get him sacked for unprofessional and unethical behaviour,' but the dean knew this would only add fuel to the fire. Instead, we arranged an anti-bullying workshop, and all staff were told to attend. During the workshop introduction, Senior Prof came into the seminar room carrying his paper-bag lunch, sat down, then stood up again. 'I have been bullied into attending this workshop,' he said, and left.

Later that year, he made a claim for months of unused annual leave dating back to the 1980s – pre-computer era, beyond record retrieval. He threatened to go public unless the faculty paid him $35,000. The university held no records to dispute his claim, and paid him out.

Early in the job, keen to bond with my office colleagues, I arranged a bit of fun at lunchtime with an absurdities and oddities tour of the gothic campus. Five of my new female workmates and I visited a museum celebrating an Australian classical music composer. The glass display cabinets were draped with leather whips and terry-towelling garments, revealing a penchant for sadomasochism. We giggled way too much and were asked to leave by the dusty curator.

Then we visited the medical museum, aghast at the collection of ancient fetuses and staring heads in glass bottles floating in spirits, lined up in stasis. Skeletons danced around our queasy lunch chit-chat and we returned to our desks shaken.

In my first year, I was assigned a special faculty-wide project. Historical 'medical' research had been undertaken for decades at the uni by academics trying to prove that Australia's First Peoples had smaller heads and brains than Europeans, and were therefore dumber. This 'research' left a lot of remains unburied and stashed throughout campus facilities. The university's shameful history was being exposed by government decree, and my mission was to report on found First Nations human remains and artefacts from this gruesome practice.

I sourced faculty building plans and mapped out my search. I looked in every closet for skeletons and searched high and low for cultural artefacts. It was spooky work, and took weeks to complete. I found one full set of bones. A kooky senior lecturer had a complete skeleton hanging off a hook and chain in his office.

'It's a leftover from the medical faculty. I'm quite fond of talking to it,' he said.

'Okey-dokey,' I said.

I lodged the remains and artefacts audit report, and several weeks later a specialist First Nations anthropologist fella came to verify the bones. 'No, these are not the bones of a First Nations Person. This skeleton belongs to a young Indian woman. The criss-cross indentations scarring her knee-bones indicate she worked long hours in fields. Indian skeletons are cheap to buy for anatomy study,' he concluded.

I felt we ought to have buried the bones of that poor Indian woman, but I could not convince the lecturer to let her rest in peace. Her small frame was left to hang in his office, his bony substitute friend.

Two years into the job in the dean's office, a new faculty general manager was appointed. The Weasel was a thirty-ish rigid Englishman with a shiny MBA. He was into mind-mapping, and what he mapped out was madness. He couldn't wait to slash and burn admin staff positions to balance the budget. The Weasel started the job the week I went on leave. By the time I got back, he'd collected pages of informal complaints about my behaviour.

To demonstrate that I was willing to change, I enrolled myself in an executive assistant's workshop held at the uni. The facilitator was on our side; she told us to act out the EA's motto, 'firm, friendly and fair' at all times. This was much more useful than being told to be 'nice'.

There was one goth woman who didn't say a word during the day-long course. I loved her reserve and her dark looks, and wanted to meet her. Ms B and I hung out after the course over lunches, then Friday nights for off-campus drinks, and later at her house, which we dubbed the devil's nest. We became solid friends. Ms B was executive assistant to another female professor who was good mates with my professor, and we'd compare notes on how tough it was for women in leadership roles and their assistants. Ms B also had a shit manager with a nasty inferiority complex who bullied her for showing up his incompetence. After Ms B found a better job to go to, she accidentally sent an email to a staff list about having to leave because of 'little man'. After she frantically tried, and failed, to retrieve the message through her mates in the IT department, Little Man read the email. Not even realising it was about him, he deleted it as spam.

At the end of every year, the entire faculty would head off-campus to a coastal resort for an overnight staff retreat. I'd organise the whole shebang and reluctantly attend to take reams of notes in review of the year, outlining points for annual plans that rarely saw the light of day. In 2002 I wriggled out of the retreat, happy to mind the fort. On their return, I was called into the dean's office. Prof Bea looked uncomfortable as the Weasel outlined more pages of complaints.

'Everyone at the retreat agreed that you have a bad attitude, that you are the problem in the faculty. Kristine, we have decided that you need to be a blank exterior for the dean's office,' said the Weasel.

'What do you mean, blank exterior?'

'Don't express any ideas or opinions, don't show any facial expressions, don't roll your eyes, don't frown, and don't make any comments about anything. Otherwise, you will be terminated.'

'A blank exterior might be fine for a mime artist or a professional poker player, but how can I do my job if I can't express myself? Get a robot!' is what I didn't say.

'I don't know what to say, because if I say anything you have just threatened to sack me,' is what I did say.

'Now don't be silly about it,' said the Weasel.

I was in one of those no-win situations they told us about in workshops with titles like 'Dealing with Difficult People'. To keep my job, I put on a blank exterior to see how it would play. One day I had to interrupt a meeting to pass on an urgent message to a lovely professor. When he saw my expressionless dial, I scared the shit out of him.

'What's happened to your face, are you sick?' he said.

'Nah prof, it's just my p-p-p-p-poker face,' I said.

This crazy directive got me angry and I soon became the opposite of a blank exterior. I rolled my eyes like there was no tomorrow, I gave cheek to everyone, and I showed contempt towards the Weasel every chance I got.

In March 2003 President Bush declared the invasion of Iraq, he called US ally countries to form a 'coalition of the willing'; against university policy, I sent an email to all faculty staff. It read, 'If you want to be part of the coalition of the unwilling, join us for a massive protest at city square. Meet us at 5 pm in the atrium, get your peace signs ready!' At first, I received enthusiastic replies from left-leaning colleagues. Then I got an email from a lecturer who was inflamed; he wanted Australia to join the war, and he put in a complaint to the dean. History tells us how that war washed up.

By 2005, the faculty budget was deep in deficit and the dean's plan was to cut salary expenditure by offering voluntary early retirement packages to a couple of the old, expensive troublemaker professors. Meanwhile, the Weasel and some of his colleagues undertook an internal review to cut admin staff positions (which mainly involved leaving early on Fridays to get on the piss at the uni staff club and slag off their underlings). It was bloody obvious to the admin staff that they were going to shaft us one by one, starting with the easiest targets: two student services administrators. Their review concluded that the faculty needed an urgent restructure, a redesign of all admin jobs, and they told us that most of us were 'superfluous to needs'.

They advertised our expanded positions at a lower rate of pay and told us to apply for our re-jigged jobs. I reported them to the dean for unprofessional conduct. Prof Bea proceeded with admin annihilation, as not one academic had put up their hand to take early retirement. There is no official age to retire for academics.

If they don't make Emeritus Professor, they just keep hanging around like shit on a blanket.

One day during this upheaval, I crossed paths with an old foe from the bush uni. Helen the Destroyer was a faculty boss whose speciality was slashing school budgets. In the late 1990s, she was responsible for cancelling the bush university's successful undergraduate music program. Under her cut-throat direction, I was tasked with phoning the commencing music students to tell them their course offer was cancelled, as there would be no more music studies at the bush uni.

'Kristine, how wonderful to see you,' she said, lunging in for a hug as I stepped back.

'Oh, hi, what are you doing here?'

'Just a bit of part-time admin work. It's a bit lonely at home, the girls are at uni and prof husband travels, you know.'

'Why don't you put your feet up, do something else besides work?'

'Like what?'

Helen the Destroyer had never contemplated her life without work. She didn't know who she was outside of her professional persona. She was much more pleasant descending the ladder as an admin worker than she ever was ascending it as a foul faculty manager. Roles seem to take over who we are, hijacking our personalities. When we get sacked or retired, it causes an identity crisis. Unemployed means unpopular, unwanted and useless. For Helen, any old crappy office job at a university made her feel better about herself, and it was better than being at home alone.

'We must catch up for lunch one day soon,' she said.

'Bye,' I said, vowing never to be like Helen the Destroyer.

By late 2005 I was hanging in at the university but I felt sick every day. I thought it was stress. My skin erupted, I had nausea, night sweats, and I felt exhausted. A warm morning shower, toast, juice, and a couple of coffees and cigarettes before work wasn't cutting it. Something was wrong.

I had monitored a diagnosis of hepatitis C, which I'd had for ten years, when I found out I was chronically ill with liver disease. My old heroin using days had caught up with me. My wise GP advised me to get it treated before liver cancer set in. Back then, the hep C treatment was experimental to work out how long it takes to clear the stubborn virus. The medical program on offer was designed to determine at what strength and length the combination treatment needed to be for the most effective health outcomes. My GP told me the treatment was free, and I was a prime candidate.

It was a medical lottery draw that put me on the twelve-month course of interferon and ribavirin starting in spring 2006. When I asked the caring liver clinic nurse what to expect, she said, 'We've taken some tough men off this treatment because they couldn't cope. You'll be right.'

After twelve weeks of weekly immune stimulator injections into my stomach fat and daily tablets of a rugged retroviral drug, I felt like I had the flu every day. I dragged myself into the office.

My skin sprouted red lumps which turned into running, bleeding sores, all over my legs, in my groin, down my arms, covering my chest and breasts. The psychological side-effects included no memory, no verbal filters, and mood swings, from rage to crying fits. I morphed into a psychotic executive assistant.

I cleared the virus by week twelve, which the clinician said was unusual. But by the time the side effects kicked in it was too late to stop the twelve-month long treatment. I had committed to their research program, that was the deal. I was well supported over the course of the drug trials by the public hospital-based research program. They took weekly blood tests and made regular dermatology and psychiatry appointments for me. The liver clinic referred me to a psychiatrist to help me deal with my rising sadness and madness. The shrink, a kind fellow with a pointy Freudian beard, was empathetic when I told him my horror health story and doubled my dose of antidepressants.

I mentioned to Prof Bea that I had some medical issues and I was seeing a doctor, otherwise I kept the treatment secret. If anyone at work found out, they'd ask me how I got the liver disease. They'd guess it was hep C, then figure out I was an old injecting drug user, and I would have been a goner. I struggled on at work because I had no idea how bad it was going to get, and besides, I needed the money.

I lost my mind–mouth coordination, and my emotions lived on the surface. Everything I was thinking or feeling gushed out of my fat trap, followed by tears and apologies. In the faculty corridor mid-conversation about some admin matter, I would change the subject and weep for my Jewish colleague, for what was done to her people in the Second World War. In the photocopier room I told a lecturer to 'fuck off!' after she teased me about sharing a room at the next staff retreat. I said sorry and she said, 'Not to worry Kristine, I'm used to you.'

I kept going to work as I was hit with the worst of the side effects listed on the interferon and ribavirin info sheets, plus every side effect from the antidepressants and antibiotics I was also on. I took a few hours of approved sick leave here and there for regular doctor appointments, hospital blood tests and shrink sessions. I was scared I'd lose my job if I took too much leave. I sure as hell didn't want to be unemployed again.

When you are an older worker, losing your job is terrifying. It's highly likely that it will be your last, which means you're facing years on the dole. For older women like me, once you leave the workforce you've got little chance of re-entry. You may land back down the bottom of the pile at an entry level, part-time contract role, if you're lucky. When I got sicker on the job, thanks to the treatment, it was one of the worst times of my life. Some days I didn't know how I was going to make it.

In late 2006, while in the death throes of my executive assistant job and crook as a dog from the hep C treatment, I applied for other roles at the uni. I'm not sure how I did it, but I landed a personal assistant job in the sciences. Some say it's the back door of the university.

On my first day in the job, I asked my boss to explain his research in mainly man-land astrophysics.

'So, what is it you're working on, Professor?'

'Kristine, we are looking for what makes up matter.'

'Righto, just asking in case I need to know.'

As his PA, I would open Professor Matter's mail, date stamping and prioritising it for a response in our morning meetings.

'I have a couple of long letters here, handwritten by a fundamentalist Christian I think, they only signed with their first name. He reckons you are going to hell for your devil's work, and he believes that you are mistaken, because he has proof that our universe is created by the almighty God. How would you like to reply?' I asked.

'Put that one with the others in the "Nutters" folder, it's on the shelf above your desk,' said Prof.

'But they say that you are going to die, doesn't that count as a threat?'

'We're all going to die, Kristine. There are hundreds of letters like it on file, I've been getting them for years. It's okay, I don't believe in them either.'

He was too busy with the Hadron collider, smashing atoms and hypothesising his head off, to worry about religious wackos.

I worked under the critical eye of a manly school manager, recently divorced and newly lesbian, and Big Red, her sour, ginger sidekick and devoted mini-manager in waiting. The school manager treated us like disobedient children, yelling out, 'Answer that phone!' after one ring. A few weeks into me starting the new job, Big Red filled in for two days while the manager was at a conference. Day one, Big Red accused me of not showing up to work; I'd taken an approved sick leave day. Day two, she picked a fight with me over which shade of blue card to put on a noticeboard. She reported me the minute the manager got back.

I finally applied for indefinite sick leave, starting with six months paid leave supported by a letter from the hospital and a doctor's certificate stating I was unfit for work. Big Red was delighted, but the manager was not happy. She asked me if I was contagious.

Late 2006, before I started my paid sick leave, the school manager insisted I go to the sciences Christmas party. She bragged all day about Big Red's incredible singing voice. 'She was the karaoke star of the party last year, you'll enjoy yourself,' she told me.

I was in no mood for a work do. The party was held in the staffroom on the sixth floor with flat beer, warm wine, chips and a karaoke machine. I got drunk and went into karaoke battle with Big Red. She was hogging the microphone, singing Dolly Parton's '9 to 5', loving herself sick. Next minute, the Bee Gees classic, 'Staying Alive', popped up. I snatched the mic off Big Red and sang like a banshee, dancing in circles like a disco fool until I wrapped the mic cord around my legs and got stuck to the spot.

I spent most of 2007 at home alone on extended sick leave, attending regular hospital and psych appointments. By late 2007, I was slowly getting better, seeing friends again, celebrating my functioning liver and going out to see bands, to have a dance and a few drinks. I was feeling like my old self, and I was flat broke. I hoped to go back to my job in the sciences office.

In December, I attempted to return to the job part-time. But by the fifth day back, Big Red had put in a formal complaint against me. 'She rolled her eyes and didn't say good morning,' whined Big Red. That old chestnut.

The school manager called me into her office and said, 'Your absence has affected your performance.' I couldn't argue with that. I'd been on approved sick leave for a year. No-one wants an unwell, ageing woman back on the job, and I was too worn down to fight back. I had to choose whether to stay and fight for a job I didn't really want, or just go.

My good mate Beth was visiting town that week. Beth was my guardian angel, a dear friend who stood by me through it all. She had gone north after her faculty restructured her out of her job. Beth calls me the Vogon Whisperer. Vogons are hideous bureaucratic monsters in *The Hitchhiker's Guide to the Galaxy*. Like Beth, I can work around just about any hellish managerial creature or senseless admin system to make shit happen.

But back at my desk with no paid leave left and a complaint on my first week back, I sent my resignation email to the manager, effective immediately. One minute later I received an email from her telling me I was sacked and advising me that I could lodge a formal equal opportunity complaint if I wished. She knew full well she was in the wrong.

Seconds later, the manager called me into her office again and shut the door.

'I suppose you can't be bothered doing anything about this?' she said.

'Didn't you see my email? I quit,' I said.

She was visibly relieved.

I'd be buggered if I was going to give them the chance to lure me during a lengthy equal opportunity process. Quitting felt good for a moment, but I knew it would delay my unemployment benefits claim at Centrelink. I just couldn't stand being sacked for being sick and on approved leave. I wanted to burn bridges.

It was after 5 pm so most of the sciences staff had left the building. I packed some stolen stationery into a box and tucked it under my arm, swung my handbag over my shoulder and walked down the corridor towards the university's back door, high on my career suicide. I felt better than I had in ages.

Throughout my working life, I had attended dozens of human resources workshops, full of mumbo-jumbo about maze mice reaching cheese, coloured parachutes and sharpening saws. There was a long line of private training consultants busting to tell the uni bosses about these latest people management tools. Shut in a room, seated in a circle, bouncing balls and role-playing, we participated out of fear for our jobs. Any one of us could be singled out as the team misfit. We lied on suspect personality tests in order to align to the best possible type, assigned like a birthmark.

I remember when Professor Bea, the faculty dean, was told to conduct a 360-degree review. It spun her out. She was advised by some external management consultant to seek anonymous feedback from her colleagues, via a confidential questionnaire, about her performance. This included jealous profs, sycophantic managers and nervous admin subordinates. Prof Bea did not like the feedback she received. Some thought she was aloof and unavailable. Then the dopey consultant hounded her into embracing an 'open-door policy'. In response, we left her office door partially ajar.

The dean was also told to wander the corridors several times a week to check in with staff. This creeped her, and everyone else, out. She had no time for posturing and none of us wanted her to check up on us, especially the faculty general manager. We called her the Teflon Queen, because she really knew how to slide the work off her desk and into the lap of a worker down the line, taking credit along the way. It was the Teflon Queen's sport to put additional pressure on the hardest working staff. She used to say, with a laugh, 'If you want something done, give it to a busy person,' like that was supposed to make us feel better.

Some of the worst of the worst middle managers I encountered in the university sector were the wannabe academics. They had achieved a PhD in whatever, but settled begrudgingly into an admin management position, falling short of a career in research and teaching. With an oversized, overeducated ego, they believed operational work was beneath them. They'd spend most of their time swanning about sucking up to academics and senior management. They'd arrange useless staff training programs and in-house workshops with titles like 'Managing Up' or 'How to Manage your Manager'. They were asking us to manage them. They were unmanageable management maniacs.

The training consultants often touted the human resources bible, *The Seven Habits of Highly Effective People.* The only thing I recall from these overpaid time-wasters was something about workforces being interdependent. We were told we were valued, but it cuts both ways. What they really meant was, they needed us and we needed our jobs, so we'd better be prepared to do what they say.

It was up-close surveillance, and staff regularly struggled to fit into a constantly changing workplace. Human resources management began to bypass collective bargaining, instead dishing out individual blame and shame and encouraging personal growth. I wanted to have that malignant personal growth removed.

Then there were the workplace reviews where they asked us to 'tell us how you really feel' about your role, position, bosses and organisation. As an old-school admin worker, it was uncomfortable revealing my true feelings, admitting that I just wanted them to let me be to do the work, and pay me. When I did tell them how I really felt, it got me into trouble. I didn't know how to adapt to this crazed, new-age, short-term working world, and by all indications it was only going to get worse.

By 2019, the university I had worked at had divided and conquered its 17,000 employees, offering only one-quarter of them job security. My trade union mate Sarah described this in a newspaper interview as 'a kind of wholesale gaslighting exercise'. Three-quarters of their workforce were on individual, fixed-term contracts, lucky to have a job and in no position to rock the boat. Exactly what university management wanted: an insecure workforce with no collective bargaining power.

My friends who are still working in the university sector tell me that the pressure to perform is beyond what they've ever experienced. Excessive workloads, regularly reapplying for your job in the latest round of restructuring, and insecure work keeps staff combative and anxious. For my women friends who are in their late fifties working in the tertiary education sector, it is a matter of hanging in there. Frequent short-term sideways moves to fill contract roles, acting in higher positions short-term, or giving up and quitting. It is an extremely competitive and unhealthy work environment.

In the early days of my working life, the deal was simple. I appeared at 9 am Monday, worked the week and left it behind at 5 pm on Friday. The trouble was, I got really good at jobs I couldn't stand, and had to work with people I couldn't stomach. The nature of office support is to make success happen for other people, seamlessly, in the background. That is the mark of a good administrator, they told us in workshops. After so many years in office work, I found little satisfaction in doing a good job.

Also, I was sick to death of being told off for being human. Unpaid overtime was expected and increasing, and we were told to take time off in lieu of extra wages, which was impossible. 'Work smarter, not harder,' squawked the HR parrots. I had to admit that I was a colourful character in a sea of office grey. I couldn't fit myself in anymore. My mask had slipped.

During my later working life, management often said to me, 'It's not what you say Kristine, it's the way you say it,' leaving me with a personal challenge and an impossible ask. My true self is an outspoken, questioning proletariat sick with hepatitis. My work self is a thin veneer of pleasantness in tip-top condition. True self is crying in the toilets, stressed out of her mind. Work self is devoid of emotion, a genie responding to every command. In the end, I loathed my work self, petrified that it would take me over, dull me down, dampen my spirit until I became unrecognisable, a shell of a woman. That I would never find my true self again, and that my true self was worth nothing.

What more could I change about myself to keep a job? I couldn't change where I was from, I couldn't change my upbringing, and I couldn't change who I was. My big, loud working-class family had shaped my forthright communication style, and I was out of date.

It was too late for me to change, and it was too draining biting my tongue and holding back eye-rolls all day at work. I was older and wilder, and I realised that I couldn't fit myself into this new workforce anymore. Management had lured out my true self, and that meant I was no longer a suitable employee. Pretending to be a loyal, compliant worker was beyond my capacity. Landing and keeping any job would become my next challenge.

Fear of poverty in older age drove me on. I had to get more money before I was too old and would never work again. Maybe I could become a senior manager? I dry-retched at the thought of studying for an MBA. Something strange happens to people as their salaries increase and their authority rises. They seem to lose sight of where they came from, and it's lonely and competitive at the top.

While I was on extended sick leave after the hep C treatment, in between waves of depression, skin eruptions and flu-like symptoms, I thought long and hard about who else I could be, beyond an office drone. I didn't know how to earn a living doing anything else. I did not want to return to work, but I didn't know what else to do.

I kept thinking that if I put half that work effort into my creative life, maybe I'd get somewhere. Not towards money, but towards storytelling, towards creating something. I had been told to shut up for so long, all I wanted to do was speak out. I had a burning desire to write, and I figured that I just needed to keep learning how, and I would find my story. But first, I had to get well.

CHAPTER 6

Christmas turkey hotline

For twelve months I hunkered down at home on extended unpaid sick leave, to ride out the aftermath of the treatment. I discovered how sick you can feel without dying, and how being that sick for that long can make you feel like death warmed up.

Some days during the worst of the treatment I felt so sick I could barely walk upright. Isolated and out of work, I holed up in my flat. One cold, rainy day, rugged up in my woollen hat, scarf and bulky winter coat, shivering under my umbrella, I bumbled across the car park to the shopping plaza. I passed a woman standing next to a huge four-wheel drive.

'Do you want a dollar? If you take this shopping trolley back you can keep the dollar,' she said.

'What? Oh, you want me to take your trolley back. No, I have a job. I'm just really sick.'

'Well, you don't have to be like that. I was just trying to help.'

'Ah, the road to hell, paved with good intentions,' I said, turning tail for the shops without the woman's trolley.

In October 2007, I got the all-clear for the hep C virus.

'Thank god that worked,' said the liver clinic consultant.

'You're not kidding, doc,' I said.

After I finished the final doses of the treatment, the side-effects got much worse. I was deeply depressed and I scratched constantly, covered in weeping, bleeding sores. I developed an obsessive-compulsive picking disorder, tearing at my fragile skin for eight hours straight, from morning to night. I struggled to feed myself, my hair fell out, and I dropped 10 kilos.

The liver clinic doctors had warned me about my demons rearing their ugly heads during the treatment. For the first time in twenty years, I wanted to use heroin. Anything to feel nothing. Instead, I took up smoking pot again and it helped. On top of the weeping rashes and skin picking, a benign psychosis lingered like a sinister stranger. It was scary to go outside, and I had holes all over me.

I attended follow-up appointments for months with a psychologist specialising in OCD. She helped me to understand I was in a self-harming psychosis caused by the treatment. She told me my blood was not dirty, and that there were no creatures crawling under my skin that I had to pick out. We agreed that my mind was temporarily messed up. I was stuck in a loop of wrong thinking.

I was spending a small fortune on a bulk supply of bandages, only to rip them off to reopen the wounds. It was the worst time in my life, and I did not know when it would stop or how to stop it. No-one could have prepared me for the misery and self-harm I was lost to.

I continued with follow-up appointments with the dermatologists at the hospital. I felt silly because I knew that they knew my skin problems were self-inflicted. But we all said nothing.

'Nice shoes,' said one skin doctor, squatting beside me as I carefully pulled up my trouser legs, exposing scratched, inflamed skin; my bloody shame.

'Do you need another appointment?' said the other doctor, the sight of my eczema setting off his itch, looking at me like I was a scabby lab rat. He prescribed stronger steroid cream and antibiotics, and more time.

At the next appointment I was taken into a room where the doctors asked me to stand on a chair to show a couple of skin professors my ravaged exterior. Ankles to thighs deep in weeping sores, my condition impressed them.

'You'll have to stop scratching,' said the skin prof.

'Yeah, I'll do that.'

One doctor suggested bathing in saline solution. Warm salt water, Mum's cure-all, cheap and easy. I soaked in sea-salt baths at home, rinsing and oiling the life back into my cracked shell.

I headed down the coast to visit my siblings, to submerge my wounds in the sea. They were shocked to see my damaged surface. Eczema runs in our family. At night Mum would scratch until she bled. For years she smothered her red raw arms in cortisone ointment and covered them in cling wrap before bed so she could get some sleep. She'd get up to go to work at an industrial wet photocopier factory, where the chemicals inflamed her skin through cotton and industrial rubber gloves. Rinsing, rewrapping and repeating.

One day I went to the shops and locked myself out of my Northcote flat. Panicked, I bolted up High Street to a locksmith. I burst through the door in a sweat. I must have looked like the mad girl eating the grass.

'I need a locksmith now!'

The man behind the counter looked scared.

'Please sit down, calm down, and ...'

'When is the locksmith coming? I have to get back into my flat. I need to have a bath! I need to know now!'

He ushered me to the door and locked me out of the locksmith shop. I kicked at the glass door, swore and shook my fist at him, and sat crying on the footpath outside his shop. He took pity and let me back in, and half an hour later a locksmith arrived at my place. I soaked my poor skin in the bath, bawled and berated myself for being a maniac.

During my post-treatment torment, I think I also went through menopause. It was all a bit of a blur. I was already a hot, angry mess, and with my fixation on picking, I hadn't noticed that I hadn't had a period for ages. At a beach retreat to number one sister's holiday caravan in Blairgowrie, I was so out of my mind I said to her, 'I think I might be pregnant. I had sex about a year ago, but I haven't had my period since. I can't figure it out?' Sister kindly reminded me that I'd had my tubes tied, pointing out that if I was pregnant, I would have been gestating a toddler.

A few months later I had a doozy of a period. Relieved, and finally convinced I wasn't up the duff, my last cycle took my cracked mind off the ongoing psychosis for a week. The night sweats and mental morass of menopause were similar to what I was already experiencing with the after-effects of the treatment. At forty-eight I was all done, and reproductive liberation was mine.

After five years living apart, one morning walking up Separation Street in Northcote I passed Will sitting outside a coffee shop, smoking rollies and reading the newspaper. I didn't want to stop but he insisted he had something important to say to me. 'I am sorry I treated you badly when we were together,' he said, which is all I ever wanted to hear. I went on my way to work, happy.

I had just started the year-long hepatitis C treatment when we reconnected. One day Will rang me to see how I was doing. Not good, I told him. I asked him to bring me bandages to cover my wounds. Will was at my place via the chemist in twenty minutes and tenderly helped me seal my raw skin. We drank tea, smoked cigarettes and talked each other back to a loving friendship.

Within two weeks Will was diagnosed with lung cancer. I visited him the day the doctors attended his hospital bedside. It was terminal.

I leaned in close to whisper in his ear.

'I love you.'

He whispered back, 'I love you too, but if I go back to my place, I will kill myself.'

He was sharing a house with walking-dead addicts in Preston. I took Will home to my flat in Northcote and we met with two of his sisters to break the terrible news. Will was one of ten siblings, and their small commission house was full. In a couple of weeks his sisters arranged for a bedroom to be free back at their family home.

Will was there for me throughout some of the darkest and loneliest months of my treatment. All through his rounds of chemo and radiotherapy I was there for him too. But I was getting better and he was only ever going to get worse. The cancer treatment made Will's legs turn blue, and his whiskers too, while my legs turned red with uncontrollable eczema. What a shining spirit Will was to me, no matter how sick he was. He comforted and counselled me as I slowly went mad on the treatment, along with my eldest sister, who supported me like a second mum, as she had always done.

Will wanted to live longer, but it was too late. The doctors told him six months, and he lasted twelve. In his final year we had the most fun we'd ever had together. We spent time with his big family and his beautiful daughters, visited friends, went to high tea, danced to bands, walked out on lame movies, and saw *Keating: The Musical*. We laughed our heads off. We got drunk, smoked weed and when he couldn't draw breath anymore, I baked pot into chocolate brownies. We lived like there was no tomorrow.

Out of work, I had been living on credit for months. Each month, to meet my payment, I'd take a cash advance from the credit card to make the repayment, spiralling into more debt. One freezing winter day in 2008, desperately scouring my Uni Super statements, I discovered that I was covered for salary insurance due to illness. Quick as lightning I filled in the forms. The paperwork looked like a mad woman's breakfast; white-out and pen rewrites scribbled my sorry story, and history was on my side.

Back in 1999, as I neared the end of my contract in continuing education at the bush uni, I worked for a good-for-nothing boss – a cast-off from the university who spent his working days reading newspapers and driving around in his uni car waiting for a redundancy package. He wouldn't sign off anything until it was way past the deadline. He was, as we say in the admin world, my stressor. One day, the head of the bush university's HR department, a decent fellow, rang to ask me if I was willing to dob in my boss for neglecting his duties. I said yes, and he soon left with a large payout.

Eight years later, somehow Uni Super made sense of my claim and I got paid $8000 from my income insurance. It was a miracle. I paid off some credit card debt and had money to spend. Then I noticed who had signed off my claim. It was that same HR boss that I had helped out as a whistleblower back at the bush uni. Thanks to super-man, I would live again.

If I learnt anything during those sickly months, it was a renewed compassion for myself and anyone who has a long illness, a disability or depression. Skin holds memories in scar tissue, reminders of old wounds. When your skin is torn, you see your flesh and blood, a vulnerability you can't hide. You are turned inside out. By the time I surfaced from the skin-picking OCD, a permanent history was etched into my outer layer.

It took some time to shake off the feeling that I was the walking wounded. Eventually, I regained mental stability, and my health returned. One year to complete the treatment and another year to get over the horrendous side effects. It took much longer to get over that treatment than it took to get over my narcotics addiction.

On the advice of my psychologist, I kept a skin-picking diary.

1 September 2007

9 am: Get up, wrap on a sarong, strip sheets off the bed and spray yellow and red leaks with stain remover, put on a load of washing. Avoid looking down or in the mirror. Peel back bandages, scabs lift and leaks start again. Inspect worst groin, leg and breast sores. Promise not to pick all of them. Dab leaking skin with cotton pads, clear liquid flows and blood oozes as I press around the skin openings. Blood inkblots onto dozens of tissues. Relief when I see the blood stop flowing, rebandage.

1 pm: Shower stings open spots, pat dry with blood blotched towel for the washing. Stick 35 sensitive skin band-aids over holes, hold tissue over big gushers because band-aids won't stick, wash hands again. Eat toast, drink coffee, hang out sheets and towels, watch TV, smoke cigarettes, dab at leaks running down my legs. It won't stop.

8 pm: Soak for 20 minutes in warm bath of Epsom salts and lavender oil. Bandage up again, aching all over. I smoke a joint, my skin feels better sealed out of my reach. Eat toast, smoke more pot. Inject hep C treatment drug into stomach fat and take antiviral tablet, antidepressants, and antibiotics.

2 am: I fear I may never stop picking. I want to make it heal faster but I am just digging deeper holes. My hands are numb and my back and neck ache. I take Panadol, howl myself to sleep and dream of clear, smooth skin. How on earth am I going to get back to work?

Weirdly, that skin-picking diary renewed my thoughts of becoming a writer.

Office work had been my saving grace in some ways. But like OCD, the robotic repetition does do your head in. I wanted to stop work to see what else was out there. Not like those magazine articles about a perfect family who quit their high-paying jobs to move to the south of France to grow grapes and live happily ever after on an inheritance. Something had shifted in me. Call it unemployment or a career break, I couldn't see myself going back to office work ever again. But the rent and bills had to be paid. I had to somehow find a way to stop work from sucking the life out of me, to find time and energy for my wellbeing, and to restart my creative practice.

When I was working, my writing had faded into the background. My graphic novel and half-finished short stories gathered dust under my bed. Over the years, I had been to heaps of writing workshops and visited galleries to gaze at art. The dream of earning a living out of what you love to do is for a select few. For the well-off who choose it, or the poverty-stricken who die for it. The twisted stereotype of the starving artist did not appeal to me. I knew what I wanted to be now I had grown up. I just didn't know how to make it happen.

It was a stinking hot summer at the end of 2006 and I was scratching for money and any kind of work. My old mate Will swung me some bits and pieces. I earned loose change stuffing envelopes and stapling raffle ticket books at home for $5 an hour.

Then I hit the jackpot. One day of work answering phones for a turkey help hotline at Christmas Day rates. The supplier's instructions on the frozen turkey packaging, how to safely thaw and roast the giant bird, were out by hours. The company hired a crack team of desperate casuals at double-time pay to answer phone calls from puzzled cooks Australia-wide. I had never cooked a turkey in my life. They gave us the correct defrosting instructions and a few roast turkey recipes. The phones ran hot.

I received a call from an old duck in her eighties whose sister-in-law had told her to roast a five-and-a-half kilo turkey for Christmas lunch.

'I managed to get the turkey in the oven, but now that it's cooked, I can't lift it out of the oven. What am I going to do?' she said, close to tears.

'Call your brother and tell him and his wife to come over to help you get the turkey out. Then tell your sister-in-law she'll be cooking the turkey next year.'

'Thank you love.'

Then I picked up a call from a First Nations woman from Yeppoon in Queensland about cooking a bush turkey a mate had given to her.

'I've never cooked a turkey and I feel real silly ringing up to ask,' she said softly.

'You feel silly? How do you reckon I feel spending Christmas Day working on a turkey help hotline!'

I gave her instructions by weight, temperature and time, but it got complicated.

'How about I pluck it and chuck it on the fire for a couple of hours, then see if it's cooked?'

'Good idea, do that.'

That six-hour shift paid $150 and things were looking up. My family ragged me mercilessly when I joined them that evening for our family Christmas at Mum's retirement village unit. They served me up a plate of cold turkey.

As kids we used to watch a 1960s US game show on our black-and-white TV called *Video Village*. It was a human board game with three streets lined with cardboard cut-out houses. Two teams played with two contestants each; one partner rolled a huge dice on the sidelines and players advanced in golf carts. Any time a player landed on a square that their opponent was on, they could either take an extra turn or force their opponent to return to the start.

Video Village was exactly what my mum's retirement village was like to me. Prefabricated mobile homes, one or two bedrooms, on tiny blocks with a strip of lawn, a garden bed below a front verandah, and a narrow carport down one side. The units were made in a factory in two halves and clad in plastic weatherboards, joined on site and fastened to a concrete slab.

The village was built on reclaimed land that was once the Reservoir rubbish tip. Residents used bottled gas and owned their houses, but not the land. The neat village streets wound around more than one hundred units, porches painted brown, blue or grey, with gnomes, bird baths and azaleas on display. It was affordable, close living, crawling with motorised scooters and wheelchairs. It was promoted as a leisure park offering independent living for the sixty- to ninety-year-old residents, who all got along, except for when they didn't and on-site management would step in.

Number one sister helped her fit it out with new furniture and curtains. The slimline interior walls and open-plan design made the units appear bigger inside – except for those occupied by the old ducks who couldn't part with their oversized family furniture, leaving narrow paths and a trip down memory lane. Mum said it was the best place she had ever had of her own.

Women far outnumbered men. Everyone knew everyone's business. A couple of old ducks ran an in-house lotto draw, and weekly bingo was popular up at the community hall where we'd hold our big family events. Strangers thrown together in later life became good friends and confidants, spilling the gossip on each other's families to their own. Neighbours would look out for each other, unless they were feuding, or it was their turn to go off in an ambulance. Conversations revolved around medical appointments and the rapidly changing conditions of old age. There were regular funerals and wakes to attend for a feed and a catch-up. For the younger seniors, it was their last chance for independent living in a leisure park. For the older residents it was dubbed God's waiting room.

The small village formed on top of a tip, reclaimed by women as their safe place to rest, it was quiet and floral. It became their whole world, on their own but not alone.

In the new year I was back churning out office job applications. I didn't know what else to do. I landed six interviews and no job. I'd been for three interviews at the university, but they wouldn't have me back. I faced long-term unemployment, growing debt and the threat of homelessness.

I went up to the Preston Centrelink office to apply for an unemployment allowance. I was greeted by a thirty-ish public servant at reception. He asked me some questions and entered my answers on his computer.

'You have a major violation,' he said, reading from the screen.

I shat myself. 'What is this "major violation" about?'

'Because you resigned from your job, you have a major violation according to the government's rules. You are flagged as a failure.'

'Don't talk to me in that language!'

He turned red and stepped away from the counter, clinging to his keyboard.

'Anyway, I haven't even signed on yet so you can't flag me as a failure just because I left a job. Tell me, how do I correct this vi-o-lation? Do I go back and ask them to sack me to meet your requirements?'

'There will be no payment for eight weeks because your application has to be sent to a committee in Canberra to consider waiving the eight-week waiting period, because you left your job.'

'How long will the committee decision take?'

'Eight weeks.'

I thumped my fist on the counter. He gave me a business card with a number to call.

'Here, you need to call the Centrelink hotline. They'll tell you how to proceed,' he said, glad to see the back of me.

As I turned around holding the little card, the conga line of customers waiting behind me let out a cheer and a round of applause. I left before I was escorted out the door by a large security dude.

Walking to the tram stop, I saw a wall with graffiti. It read 'useless old cunt'.

Eight weeks later, I returned to Preston Centrelink for a second crack because I had not received any money. I lined up in the unsavoury concrete office block, behind middle-aged women, labourers, ageing migrants, single mums, First Nations teenagers and newly arrived refugees. We were all superfluous to needs.

I presented with a good haircut wearing a long, crimson leather coat I had bought with one of my last pay cheques. The Centrelink officer looked me up and down, squinting at my handsome overcoat.

'Assets?' he said.

'None,' I said.

He kept eyeing my coat, which I would sleep in if I couldn't pay my rent. He then insisted I needed to do an assets test, which I did because I didn't want to end up homeless living in that coat. When the unemployment payment came through after twelve weeks, it covered one month's rent.

Centrelink's mutual obligation rules also meant that I was required to attend weekly appointments with a case manager, my employment consultant. Twenty-five-year-old Myra was with the Salvation Army job network in depressing Preston. She foretold my fortune.

'Kristine, I can see you have a bright future. It is your destiny to get another job,' she said.

'Work is a necessity, Myra. If I don't work, I don't eat.'

'How about twenty hours a week working for Centrelink?'

I'd be working for less than the dole.

'No, thanks Myra. I'd rather hawk my fork up the High Street than work for Centrelink.'

'You are funny Kristine, now sign this new activity agreement. You must apply for ten jobs every fortnight, and participate in workshops to improve your CV-writing skills, grooming and presentation, and your interview technique. Report back weekly to me on your progress.'

She told me to look at the job noticeboard on my way out. I stared at cards pinned to the corkboard, the wanted ads: labourers, factory piece workers – must have experience – telemarketing call centre shifts in the middle of the night, $15 an hour in Mernda. Cheered by an unemployment line, forced to search for unsuitable work, offered a job at Centrelink: what a day!

Fulfilling my job search agreement meant receiving numerous rejection letters for jobs that I did not want, had no hope of getting and that paid a pittance. I attended job-seeker workshops for months. They told me I was overeducated, code for 'too old'; that I needed to dumb myself down, code for 'too bright'; dye my hair and wear more make-up, code for 'not pretty enough'. It was demoralising and humiliating.

I lived my non-working life at low cost, staying home, reading, writing, doing yoga, eating in, juggling bills and rent, and racked up more debt on my credit card. I walked to the park, watched TV and DVDs, laughed, cried, applied for ten more jobs, and waited for something to happen. Office work had changed; suddenly it was considered to be a worthwhile career by young graduates and post-graduates who competed for basic admin jobs. I couldn't get a look in.

By the early twenty-first century, everyone was required to do office work as part of the new, improved computerised workplace.

Doing as I was told back in the early 2000s, I had helped to develop and roll out university-wide web-based systems. Admin tasks went online; I had unwittingly assisted in the elimination of my all-rounder office role. At first, it was funny to watch the academics freak out at having to enter student marks into a database system. At least they still had a job: mine.

University photocopier rooms filled with tutors, lecturers and professors who gained PhDs in copying and collating. It made no economic sense, and none of us were happy about it. Then electronic personal assistant systems helped bosses to organise their own meetings using online calendars, struggling with schedule clashes and fighting over block-bookings.

There were also far fewer ongoing salaried positions and a lot more applicants competing for contract jobs. There were more project consultants than you could poke a stick at. Shitloads of graduates were gagging to enter the university workforce; carrying massive course fee debts, they were desperate for paid work. They'd take anything.

Then handheld digital devices and mobile phones changed the workplace landscape forever. Dedicated admin assistant jobs evaporated into the ether. Before many white-collar workers realised it, a technology-driven paradigm shift had happened. Human interface workers were being made redundant en masse across the globe. Then flexible work arrangements, which sounded great, morphed into ridiculous split-shifts, disjointed part-time hours across several jobs, and being on call 24/7 via mobile phones and email. Opportunities for women to progress declined as we took on more fixed-term and part-time work.

Maternity and carer leave absences kept women at the back of the pack, and old ducks like me were *so* twentieth century.

Our twenty-first century lives and our workplaces became complicated, and controlled by computers. Executives interfaced with machine logic and distanced themselves from awkward human workforce management. Computer systems began to have a greater say over workers than their bosses, who became low on empathy, high on staff turnover, and obsessed with data. The latest software started to monitor the output of workers, and increasing productivity became the be all and end all.

Robotics began to rule blue-collar workplaces. Process workers were expected to emulate and keep up with their robot bosses. No talking, no sitting down on the job, no matter what human needs may arise. Piss in a bottle if you have to, just don't stop working! Computer systems became the boss of us and this let the human bosses off the hook.

Siri became the ultimate subservient assistant. Siri is a digital Girl Friday who doesn't talk back. She sounds female but her answers are coded by some slavish, droll nerd. If you ask Siri 'what are you doing later?' she replies, 'I'm at work. My shift ends in 614,978 years.' Siri took my job and she is programmed to never retire. How can I compete with that?

Futurists predict that workplace computers will be programmed to know much more about us than we need or want them to know. Like automatically docking your pay when you leave your desk for extra trips to the toilet due to stress incontinence, induced by the fear of losing your job if you take too many toilet breaks. Robotics are also getting intimate with the elderly, thanks to the invention of battery-powered robotic pants. There go the jobs for human caregivers, and more urine-related issues. But who is going to remove and repair them when they short-circuit after an accident? Another robot?

I continued to live in hope that new-century workers would return to trade unionism, united in solidarity to fight against the demands of machines. I dreamed of a fed-up rank and file coming together to organise and resist the commands of robots and their remote masters. An epic sci-fi struggle of good over evil, connecting via internet toasters at clandestine brunch meetings to resist and rise up, to demand equal pay for all workers, and to humanise the workforce again. But, like my working life, my dream was fading fast.

The utopian ideal of a futuristic world promised workers that dirty, dangerous and dull jobs would be done by automatons. But without enough work for everyone, what on earth are humans going to live on? Maybe we'll all become data miners for Google? Or maybe we won't have paid jobs at all, just endless leisure time to drool and scroll. But how are we going to afford the power and data to stay online? Maybe I ought to look into retraining as a robotic pants technician. It's a dirty job, but someone has to do it.

But I knew I had to arrange for workforce re-entry if I was to navigate unrecognisable workplaces and survive an uncertain future. There was no way I could stay alive on the dole and in debt for much longer. I had never felt so desperate for work, and every potential employer could smell it.

The indignity of being unemployed had left a stink of desperation about me. Work clothes frayed at the edges, shoes scuffed and heels worn, my professional image had seen better days. My skin condition worried me constantly, my eyes welled with fear, my face was pained with depression. I was not the picture of health and far from a sunny new employee keen to get back to work. Forget decent pay rates, I would have taken any job on offer.

CHAPTER 7

That's not the deal

BY JULY 2007, I had been unemployed for more than six months when I landed a full-time, ongoing job as an administrator for a welfare organisation. I had been searching for a full-time admin role with a not-for-profit since I left the uni sector. I'd spend my days at home scouring the internet and newspapers for vacancies with decent wages and doable position descriptions. Any old job that would hire an old unemployed duck like me. I was rapt to get a look in for any job, I was so broke I would have worked anywhere. I found the admin job in my local newspaper and got the sense that this was an old school workplace with traditional values, so I dusted off my office mask and attempted to fit in.

'Tell us about yourself, Kristine,' said the nutty white-haired fella at the interview. He was boss of the unit. Professor Bea, from my last job, had given me a glowing reference, bless her.

'I'm really keen on this position. I'm an administrator, no shame in that,' I said.

It was a rusty reply but I hadn't been interviewed in a while. I also knew I needed to dumb myself down for the low rate of pay on offer to avoid the ageist, 'you seem too experienced for this job' get-out clause. But I got the job because I had skills and experience way beyond what they needed. I was also willing to work for crumbs. They offered me an annual salary of $38,000. I copped a $20,000 pay cut. I had to get back to work and they knew it. I sucked up the backwards step, dreaming of a beach holiday on North Stradbroke Island. My rent and bills would be covered, I'd buy name-brand food, I'd go out with friends, and I'd buy a bag of pot. I could pay off my credit card. Maybe the money would last ten years and I could afford a future.

I was a nervous wreck returning to work. It reminded me of my first day as a Girl Friday. I spent a lot of time in the toilets re-bandaging remnant leg sores and praying to get through the day without any leaks. On day two of my new job, white-haired Prof told me he was surprised to see me; apparently the last woman didn't come back after her first day. From my first-floor office window I noticed a mini-van parked across the street with a bed sheet draped over it. It had a hand-painted message that read, 'They sacked me unfairly. They are supposed to help people. Now I am poor.' Not a good sign.

My role was supporting the Prof and his team doing low level office admin including reception, new staff inductions, ordering office supplies, making sure the photocopier was working, taking minutes, co-ordinating and promoting events, and picking up food for frequent farewells. I also did regular shifts on the main office reception dealing with people in crisis, hungry addicts, and chatty elderly day centre visitors. At first, the job was manageable, but I was well aware of the high staff turnover.

I was a few weeks into the new job when my dearest Will died.

I visited Will often towards the end in the palliative care ward in East Melbourne, until the glazed stare of a soul heading to the other side possessed his blue eyes and he barely recognised me. He was so ill I am not sure he knew he was dying. I knew he was close during my last visit when he shat the bed and gave me a pleading look, as if to say, 'please don't come again to see me like this'. I said my last words to him: 'A good man is hard to find.'

On a dark winter morning a few days later, Will gave up the ghost and left at dawn. I placed a death notice in his favourite newspaper, thanking him for his love and friendship. It was placed beside him in the coffin.

That sad morning, I went to work as always. One of the sweet managers, Gerry, saw there was something wrong. Lifting my head from my desk, I sobbed, 'My dear mate has just passed away.' Gerry insisted I take some time off work and I did, to howl on my couch for four days and four nights. Gerry's empathy allowed me time to grieve in private, a reprieve from supporting others, to be bereft, to be left completely alone. It allowed me time to turn off my can-do work persona. Time to take my private feelings home, and to protect my only source of income, too.

In the darkest times, we see our pain clearly in the caring eyes of others. We work through sickness and sorrow. Work is a great distraction from the harsh realities of personal upheaval hidden in the after-hours. It keeps us afloat financially when everything else around us is going to shit. Work gives us a sense that something is on track, that a better future is possible. It helps us keep our act together.

The most important act of all is when compassion is shown by colleagues, especially by bosses; when they notice our humanness, that someone is not quite right. Kindness reminds us we are human. We are not just our jobs. We are not human resources. We are human beings.

In the early days of my new job, I learnt about the language of welfare by attending the weekly seminars that I organised. I found out all about disadvantage from a theoretical point of view, and why so many of us stay poor. I could have told them myself, but no-one ever asked me. Every so often a genuinely brilliant bit of breakthrough thinking was presented. Deliberative democracy was a framework based on asking poor people what they needed and wanted to inform the delivery of support services. This was the opposite of promises driven by political intentions and election timelines, which often spent a shitload of funding but achieved no change, or left people worse off. This was common sense to me, consistent with my lived experience, but it was considered way too radical by many in the welfare sector.

Imagine people having a say in government decisions. Next thing you know they'll be successfully running their own lives!

One year into the job, my dear colleague Lisa put me forward for a pay rise. Lisa was executive assistant to the top boss, with an incredible work ethic and a mighty sense of justice. She made a strong case to my boss. Lisa told him I needed to be paid for my expertise and experience, and that I ought to be paid the same rate as the other personal assistants. I was promoted to what the job really was, office manager and PA to the Professor with a salary of $48,000 a year. While grateful for the correct money and new job title, I was worried about how much more they would expect from me.

When I started the job there were a dozen staff, half were managers. All highly educated and fascinated by the plight of poor people. I was the only admin support staff. My revised role included being a PA to the Prof, redeveloping the organisation's website, managing international and local events, preparing strategic plans and reports, staffing admin, preparing meeting papers, ordering supplies and equipment, reception, getting cakes and unjamming the photocopier.

At one conference, rounding up some hapless scholars, I quietly said to Beardy, a manager straight out of a nativity scene (but with no wisdom, no gifts and no sense of humour), that 'it's a bit like herding cats'. I got the impression that didn't get us off on the right foot.

After the Labor Party was returned to power, funding was coming out of our ears. The team doubled in size and we needed more office space. I took on the extra role of project manager for the office refurbishment. I was in charge of relocating staff during renovations and office reallocations. The shifts in territorial boundaries shook the team to their core.

One colleague who worked part-time was asked to move out of her large office to make space for a new full-time professor. During multiple office moves, the building maintenance guys lost her old desk. It was dumped by mistake. I refused to look for her desk at the rubbish tip, and she never forgave me. She was so miffed she took her long service leave and I got lumbered boxing up twenty years of her work.

On her return from leave, the maintenance men delivered ten archive boxes of her old papers to the middle of my tiny office to shred. It seemed like it was payback for the office move and losing her desk. But she didn't know me very well because I loved shredding. It was my favourite office task. Reams of important papers became dead information, beyond archiving, never to be filed again. All that past turned into streamers.

I stood for hours at an ancient, chest-high metal shredder that roared like a bulldozer, located in a corridor outside the men's toilets. A stinking odour came wafting my way, followed by a jolly chap leaving the loos.

'You know, I've got an honours degree and this is what I've come to,' I said to him.

'Really? Good job,' he said, laughing as he went on his way.

The workforce of the early-noughties had changed radically. Top heavy with management and light on admin staff aligned with utopian promises of technological change and the elusive concept of the paperless office. There was something askew with the hierarchical structure at this office. I answered to multiple layers of bosses, all asserting their authority and producing a new level of workplace pressure. I had never had so many bosses. Also, despite working in a fully computerised workplace, the team refused to do any low-level admin, so I was stuck with mountains of grunt work.

I was tasked with regularly updating the office organisational chart. The A4 landscape paper print-out was no longer wide enough to fit the top-heavy row of boxes representing the many management positions. I upsized to A3 paper and managed to squeeze in a small box, my admin position, at the bottom of the page. The diagram looked like an upside-down pyramid. Totally outnumbered, I was the lone administrator.

By early 2009 the global financial crisis was taking its toll. Workers across the world were sacked, banks were going under, and governments spent big propping up failing economies. Australia's Labor Prime Minister, Kevin Rudd, slung us workers $900 each as part of his 'stimulus package', to get us to spend our way out of a looming recession. It worked. I bought a gorgeous pair of Melbourne-made tailored dark grey trousers, and a purple herringbone waist-frilled wool jacket.

By winter 2009, work was super busy and started to get interesting. I helped to organise a jobs summit at the local Town Hall. Prime Minister Rudd and a mob of left-leaning representatives came along. I was wearing my stimulus suit when

I met the PM as he greeted us women on the registration table. It was an invite-only joint event between government, welfare agencies and universities, with high-level reps, and no unemployed people in attendance.

Word had got out on the streets that the Prime Minister would be in town. A First Nations Uncle came through the doorway asking to speak with Mr Rudd. I didn't have the heart to turn him away. Without advising the federal police, who were swarming over proceedings, I walked the local fella up to the main hall where I showed him to a seat up the back. Uncle walked straight up to the front row and sat next to Prime Minister Rudd, talking softly in his ear.

Proceedings were well underway as the summit speaker continued and unrest filled the hall. I returned to the registration table and out of nowhere the communications manager was in conniptions. She raced over, yelling, 'Get him out! You let him in, now you get him out, now!'

Uncle and I walked calmly out down the centre aisle, under the glare of 180 white VIPs, flanked by two federal cops in crumpled suits who flipped-out on their walkie-talkies trying to respond to the supposed security breach. I showed Uncle to the toilets, then made him a cup of tea. As he left, proud as punch, he thanked me and blew me a big kiss. That was a career highlight for me.

The next time I met Kevin Rudd was in the Great Hall at the National Gallery of Victoria. He was to give the keynote oration for a social inclusion event that Lisa had organised. It was a slap-up dinner in magnificent surrounds. All I wanted to do was lay on the floor of the Great Hall to stare up at the amazing stained-glass ceiling by Leonard French.

I was seated on the 'First Nations table', stuck up the back of the stage behind a pillar, with my colleague-mate Dee, a Noongar woman, and other senior First Nations community members. During the PM's speech, we passed around a piece of paper at our table, suggesting questions for Dee to put to the PM.

'For First Nations people, what do you think social inclusion would look like?' asked Dee.

The PM rattled on about fairness, and listening to elders' stories, and stuff that political replies are made of, and we listened attentively. When dessert was served, Dee, ready with a second question, walked over to Kevin's table and said to our top boss, 'Who's your mate?' We snickered around our table in the background. Top Boss introduced the PM to Dee as she showed off her self-determined social inclusion, getting a one-on-one with Australia's leader as he ate his pudding.

In my third year on the job a lame joke set off one of the managers. The photocopier was making blow-out noises when she walked by my office.

'What's that noise?' she said.

'Maybe it's you farting?' I said, foolishly.

It was a bad joke and the manager was enraged. She proceeded to gang up with the other managers to compile a list of mounting grievances against me. Soon, three pages of formal complaints were lodged with my boss and escalated up to the human resources office.

Upstairs, one big boss ruled. A tough woman sporting a distasteful eighties dress sense. Her brutal sackings were legendary. My mate Lisa and I had started at the welfare organisation one week apart. Big Boss disliked both of us equally, as she seemingly did all outspoken trade unionists. I soon found out that sometimes there is no such thing as sisterhood in the workplace. I would also discover that toxic leadership trickles down to create systemic corrosion and coercive behaviour at every level.

I had undertaken some health and safety training on the job and was the go-to person for the office. One day one of the managers asked me to provide a bucket to a heavily pregnant colleague who felt sick while sitting at her desk. Instead, I went to check on my work mate and found her ashen-faced and slumped on her manager's office floor, dry retching over a rubbish bin. I arranged for her partner to collect her from work, and reported it as an OH&S incident. Then I was reported for not doing as I was told. Here we go again. My office mask was paper thin and I couldn't hide my true self, and why the hell should I? I cared when my colleagues were unwell, isn't that what we are supposed to do?

The next day I told her manager what had happened. 'Did she vomit into my bin?' was all she had to say.

The soon-to-be mum never returned to the job. Months later, she visited me with her beautiful baby and thanked me for my help that day.

Then the Professor started to undermine me in meetings. His managers joined in, keen to ensure they were not his targets.

Before this job, Professor was a priest, he entered the workforce in his fifties, late in life. He did not have a professional bone in his body. A lovely colleague who was in the priesthood with the Professor, told me, 'He was difficult back then and he's still difficult.' The Undertaker, as the Prof was nicknamed by the organisation's elderly clients out the back of the office, was well known in scholarly circles for his overbearing ego and duplicitous behaviour. At the international conferences I managed, when visiting scholars found out that I was his PA, they would ask me, 'How do you manage him? Are you okay?'

'No, I'm not okay.'

One day my mate Dee, who sat opposite my office, overheard Prof telling me off.

'What the fuck are you doing? You don't know what you're doing!' was his standard cry.

'Hey Kristine, he can't speak to you like that, go tell his boss,' Dee said quietly after he left.

I made an appointment through Lisa and told the top boss exactly what Prof had been yelling at me. Top Boss covered his ears and was suitably appalled. He told Prof to stop it. From that meeting onwards I knew the axe would fall; I just wasn't sure who it would fall on.

By late summer 2010 I was barely hanging on at the welfare office. At my end-of-year performance review, Prof told me that some of the senior managers had complained to him that I was 'too aggro'.

'My aggression was in response to disrespectful treatment by management,' I replied.

I also told him I'd tone it down. I returned to my office and sticky-taped a sign to my computer:

'I AM NOT A HUMAN RESOURCE. I AM A HUMAN BEING.'

I continued into my fourth year in an ever-expanding role. I had only ever lasted three years in the same job. The first year in a job was new and interesting. The second year was spent getting the job down pat. By the end of the third year, I was usually juggling a heavy workload while the bosses asked for more as I was already half-way out the door.

Two days after returning from annual leave, I sensed more trouble brewing. Professor handed me a letter he had signed on behalf of the managers. It outlined their concerns about my behaviour. It was all about me being rude and loud. They could not fault my work. They got me on my upfront personality.

None of the managers noticed me buckling under the workload of three administrators. I kept pedalling as fast as I could to keep up. They didn't care that I could hardly breathe because I was drowning in admin tasks. It was unbearable being under their constant scrutiny. I had lost all credibility as a forthright, competent office manager. I hated the job and the unrealistic conditions I worked under.

This was not the deal. The deal was a fair day's pay for a fair day's work. Eight hours of work, eight hours play, eight hours sleep, that's the deal. I realised the old working world I had known was gone. Employers now wanted way too much for way too little in return, at great cost to our health, safety and sanity. What lengths would I have to go to stay in this job?

It pained me to admit that I couldn't manage the demands of the role. It was a real eye-opener. Never shy of hard work, I had taken on a mammoth workload, and my bosses had encouraged it, praised me for it. They had milked my Protestant work ethic for all it was worth, and exploited my desperate need to work.

I witnessed the promotion of complete incompetents because they were mates with the upper echelon. I watched dedicated colleagues be driven out for standing up for themselves. We used to say that the old drunks out the back of our office got better treatment than the staff at the welfare organisation. It was a do-gooder's madhouse.

During this time, my friend Lisa and I would meet each other in the women's toilets, retreating, sometimes crying, overcome by our workloads, suffering headaches and feeling sick to the stomach. At one point Lisa was so tired and stressed from her ridiculous work hours that she spilt a whole carton of burning soup over herself and ended up in hospital. We agreed we could not go on like this. Something had to give, and it wasn't going to be us.

I started skimming through the work as fast as I could just to keep up, working more and more unpaid hours. Under the threat of ongoing complaints, the whip cracked louder.

By Easter 2010, for the first time in my working life I had contacted my trade union for advice and support. A burly bloke from the community services union represented me at a formal disciplinary hearing with Prof and Big Boss in HR.

'Stay quiet for now and we'll see what they say,' he told me before the meeting started.

Big Boss informed me that if I told anyone about the disciplinary meeting I would be disciplined further, and that this would lead to my termination. They then insisted I read out loud three pages of complaints that had been lodged against me since I started the job.

The union rep said my offhand comments were not the basis for termination and that their treatment of me was unfair. He stuck up for me, then highlighted my impossible workload.

I admitted that at times I had been rude and loud, but I was pushing back against the overwhelming demands of the job.

'I'm worried that you may be trying to work me to death,' I said, only half-joking.

Professor grinned. Big Boss licked her lips.

Out of the formal complaint debacle, it was arranged for me to see a workplace coach, he was a personal friend of the Big Boss. The two-hour psychobabble session was more than I could take. He thought that my 'bad behaviour' was due to my upbringing. I agreed with whatever piffle he said.

I was then told to meet with each of the complaining managers for coffee and a chat, to apologise for my behaviour and to talk about what they expected from me.

Lily-livered Beardy reckoned he was frightened of me.

One manager saw my role as being more nurturing.

One of the ringleaders wanted more eye contact from me. I stared at her until she blinked. She also wanted me to smile at her. I grinned. She knew two management tricks: how to starve an employee of work to get them moved on, and how to overload an employee with work until they collapsed and left. Did they teach this toxic mismanagement shit in MBA programs?

One of the kinder managers, who I felt was on my side, gave me a badge from a conference that said in Swedish, 'your mother doesn't work here'.

I knew what they wanted from me. They just wanted me to be 'nice'. The problem with being nice all the time is that when you do stand up for yourself in a direct way, your concerns are dismissed because you're not being nice, and you are labelled as aggressive. They also said I was supposed to say 'yes' to every request they made, because I was being too negative when I said 'no'.

Leave me alone and let me do the job, was what I wanted to say, but no-one would listen to that. Instead, wearing my blank exterior face, I said, 'That's a good point, I'll take that on board. I will be mindful of that in future. I request we be open and honest in our communications, so we can move forward into better working relationships.' I spewed office newspeak at them to get them off my back. I couldn't win so I pretended to be exactly what they wanted, knowing that being nice was unsustainable and that I was no yes woman.

By winter 2011, I couldn't take being branded as the office problem any longer. I'd taken all the blame and had apologised to the managers and nothing had changed. I'd even paid to see a workplace psychologist after hours. She also tried to convince me that I was the problem, and that I was holding the whole office up against the wall by their throats. No mean feat given I only have two hands. She said that I should just get on with the job and grow up. She was sort of right. I realised that I had outgrown subservient admin roles, shit treatment on the job, and psycho assessments.

While I continued in the job to keep my own poverty at bay, I told myself over and over to just produce good results for the team. But I couldn't convince myself. Instead, I waited for change. I only needed another ten years of full-time employment to get me to retirement, but after only three years in the role I felt exhausted. I was in a no-win situation. Deep down, I knew I didn't want to play offices anymore.

It had gotten to the stage that any fulfilment in my role was gone. It didn't matter if I did a good job or a bad job. I was being worked into an early grave. My mental health was at risk, and all the signs were there.

At lunchtime I'd sit up the back of the offices under a gum tree, crying, smoking cigarettes and desperately praying for a way out. At home at night, nightmares of tsunamis swamped my dreams and I'd wake drenched in sweat, unable to go back to sleep. In the mornings my throat felt like it was closing up and I could hardly swallow at the thought of going into work.

Some mornings I couldn't make myself go into the office. I'd circle the building, walking around the block a couple of times, and fantasise about going back home. I'd walk past the demented elderly residents leaning over walkers, horizontal drunks, spaced-out paint-sniffers, ice heads skating and junkies scratching, bashed-in faces, blue and broken, scabbing coins for their morning fix.

Then I'd think, they got up, they got dressed, they're walking and talking and, like me, hoping for a better deal. It's a daily miracle we all keep going despite the odds, in the face of no hope and against inequity, injustice and inhumanity. Finding solace in each other, asking for help and accepting it.

On bad days I envied the simplicity of being right down the bottom again. No job, no demands. That's when I knew I was completely stressed out of my head and needed to snap back to reality.

I eventually lodged a counter-complaint against management, citing excessive workload, exploitation, and exclusion. And after one more committee meeting where Prof silenced me by shouting and banging his fist on the table, I asked to see him in his office. I shut the door and exploded.

'You can get some other poor bitch to treat like a piece of shit under your boot to do the job. I am leaving!'

'Oh, is that how you feel? But don't you need another job to go to?' he said, smiling.

I had applied for four office manager roles, got two interviews but couldn't land another job. I was trapped.

Working for such a dysfunctional workplace was too much to bear. I couldn't take any more of their noxious leadership in the guise of altruism. They were, after all, a Christian organisation and I expected fairer treatment, maybe even succour. When I first took the job, I wasn't fazed by their Christian ethos. I was christened Church of England and knew how to bullshit my allegiance to their values if it meant paid work. But what they expected from me was to do the impossible and to be grateful that I had the job. I couldn't see a way out if I couldn't land another job. With no savings left, I could not afford to be unemployed again.

Then some bright spark in HR decided to run an in-house workshop on proper grievance process and team building. A bit late, but it was designed to appease my complaint. Still hoping for change, I insisted we review the admin support needs of the growing office. I created a new trainee admin position to support the team and to help me manage the bulging workload. We appointed a young First Nations admin assistant, who was a great help. Except, like me, she didn't like office work. After six months I gave her a reference for a child care worker position and she took the job.

I gave it one last gasp in early 2012. I refocused my energy at work and turned into the events queen for the office. In addition to my regular admin duties, I organised twenty-four lunchtime seminars, six social inclusion workshops and an international symposium attracting 300 people. The events made money for their not-for-profit coffers. One day, after a lunchtime seminar in the old church out the back, I wrote on the whiteboard, 'Subvert the dominant paradigm'. Prof had a mental fit.

'Who wrote this? Did you write this Kristine? Rub it off now!'

I refused. My higher education was paying off.

By mid-2012 I felt completely stuck and I still couldn't see a clear way out. I was so busy that I didn't have time to apply for other jobs. That's when I took on a new slack work strategy.

That winter was the longest, coldest and wettest in a decade, prompting me to sleep in an extra half-hour each morning. I began getting into work later and later, arriving at the office around 11 am, unless I had an early meeting. My workmate Lisa and I took two-hour lunches, then we'd leave early, just after 4 pm. I modelled my slackness on the boss's work ethic. As long as I beat Prof into the office and scarpered just after he left, I wasn't going to get sprung. A couple of times I had to dodge him as he drove out of the car park, hiding behind the bushes near the tram stop. It was a silly ruse, but it was one way to reclaim the extra unpaid hours I had worked doing 12-hour days. It also reduced my time spent in the office.

I did the bare basics of my job, and I offered no more favours. I still got the same pay, and I was a lot less stressed. I had figured out what was meant by not working harder but working smarter. For a brief time, it worked for me. I discovered I'd been overperforming for no good reason other than the genuine fear of losing my job. I continued to underperform, I didn't make myself available, and I didn't say a word out of place to anyone. I was sure it wouldn't be long before they'd offer me a promotion!

Before I escaped, I wanted one last crack at Big Boss. She was put in charge of the First Nations strategy for the organisation after my mate Dee left for greener pastures. Dee and I had stayed in touch and I told her nothing had happened for two years with the First Nations strategy, so we cooked up a scheme to highlight the neglect.

I asked Lisa to include me on an executive meeting agenda to request an update on the First Nations strategy, even though this was way beyond my role.

'I am here on behalf of members of the First Nations community to enquire about what is happening with our First Nations strategy and action plan. It seems to have stalled since Dee left, so can I have an update to pass on to the community, please?'

Big Boss started coughing and spluttered something about the too-hard-basket, and that all the First Nations committee members were burnt out and won't come to meetings. Top Boss stopped her and asked me to continue.

'I am not sure if you are aware, but the federal government has announced millions in funding for First Nations training and employment schemes. There is money going begging and you would be mad not to apply for it,' I said, staying on message.

One of the jumped-up managers at the meeting got excited about the funding and piped up.

'We should do a project on First Nations People getting jobs, or something like that,' he said, his mouth moving faster than his one-track mind.

'Not more projects. First Nations People are some of the most studied people in this country, and still many of them can't get a look-in for a decent job,' I replied.

This was all duly noted in the minutes and, in front of the whole executive group, Top Boss told Big Boss to do her job.

It was a glorious moment of payback. As we left the meeting, Big Boss gave me a filthy look of defeat.

I took a short winter break in 2012, relaxing on the tropical beaches of North Stradbroke Island with my Mary. We stayed for a week in a '70s-era cool, white motel, walking down to a cafe and the beach by day, and across the road to the pub each night. Early evenings, basking in the northern sunlight, I would sit legs stretched out in the lapping shallows to watch the red sun set between two palmed coves, wasting time on island time.

On the mainland, Australia was about to change prime minister after some Labor party finagling. Mary was glued to her wind-up radio back at our motel room. Just as the sun went down, I saw her running along the shore towards me yelling, 'She got in, Krissy! Julia Gillard, she's our first female prime minister!' That night we celebrated our once-in-a-lifetime event and got out-loud drunk toasting our first woman in the top job.

On the island, my thoughts turned to retirement, rather than unemployment. I was hitting my early fifties with thirty-five years of work under my belt, and I'd started to think about my future beyond a job. The bulk of my working years were behind me, and like all life forms, I was running out of time. But it was weird thinking about early retirement. I knew that money would be tight, but that was nothing new for me. I was certain that I didn't want to be too fucked to enjoy myself in older age.

Back at the office, one day an old soul was sitting on a bench out the back, pulling on a fag, a milky cuppa sat between his slippers, sporting a brown faux leather jacket over his flannel pyjamas. He told me he liked my geometric coloured shirt.

'Not enough colour these days,' he said. I thanked him, sat next to him and joined him for a ciggie.

Old soul told me how he had survived three strokes, two heart attacks and a fierce post-hospital infection. He was a crusty professor, an alcoholic for twenty years, then twenty-three years ago he gave up the drink, he said. In the hospital where they'd helped to save his life, he told me about a sign on the wall: 'There is nothing in the world that will be made better by having another drink.'

We chatted about life and loss and he thanked me for listening to his words of wisdom. As he got up to go, he said, 'Be your best and the rest will take care of itself. Remember, you are here now.'

Funny how a stranger can say something profound just when you are ready to hear it. I returned to my office and calculated my projected savings up until 2020, when I would turn sixty. I wanted to see if I could afford to retire on a self-funded part-pension, around $100 a week, which I could access in a couple of years when I turned fifty-five. The unemployment allowance would cover my rent. An early work exit began to seem possible.

After attending a retirement seminar, I started to deposit every extra dollar into my superannuation, and took advantage of significant tax offsets that I had known little about. I figured out that if I lived on the poverty line and my rent doesn't go up too much, I may have just enough money to live for another twenty years. Maybe some other income would come my way. Maybe there was a way out, a chance to live beyond full-time work.

The end was in sight and I was excited. Outside of work, I rewarded myself with movies and books, healthy food, aromatic baths, yoga, walks, laughs, drinks, and hanging out with friends and family. Bit by bit I watched my super savings grow until my departure from work was in sight. I still hoped for one more decent earn before I hung up my rat-race hat.

When I finally gave my notice to the HR department late in winter 2012, I was invited to complete a confidential online exit survey. I detailed the harassment, unprofessionalism, favouritism, incompetence, and exclusion, and stated again that it was humanly impossible to meet the excessive workload of the position.

The next day, with steam coming out of her ears, Big Boss thumped into my office and demanded that I leave the building immediately.

'Are you going to pay me out for my last week of notice?' I asked.

She said yes.

'Well, if I am being forced to go early then you can stop bossing me around now,' I said as she stormed off.

After saying good luck to the stunned temp admin woman mid-handover, I grabbed my handbag, a bunch of pens, a ream of paper, and twenty post-it notepads, having recently ordered one hundred by mistake online. I was escorted to the front door of the building by a soppy HR lackey who waved me a limp goodbye.

Stepping out onto the street, I was overcome with relief. By the time I was on the tram on my way home, I faced the fact that I was unemployed again, for who knows how long, rather than in restful, secure retirement, but I didn't care. It was the beginning of the end of my office career.

I found out the story behind the mini-van protester parked outside the office on my first week on the job. His name was Aaron, a sweet fella who the Big Boss had taken a bit of a shine to when he had worked there. Sick to death of the unwanted attention, one day Aaron refused a request and she had him sacked on the spot. Big Boss also had him banned from entering the grounds of the organisation, as though he was a trespasser. Aaron told me all about this out the back of the welfare office the week I was leaving. I was not alone.

When my job title had changed to office manager, a lot of my time was spent managing my manager's unrealistic expectations of me. I experienced the worst micro-management and over-supervision ever. I was way too old for that office palaver. The much younger managers, experts in their fields, didn't have a clue when it came to office admin. They thought their job was to tell me how to do my job, and everyone wanted me as their assistant. The simple pleasure of working as part of a team of equals was gone. It seemed that we'd all become lost to vacant office speak, and everyone became a manager to get a higher rate of pay, including me.

A week after I left the welfare office, I got my final pay and leave entitlements. Most of it went to paying off debt. I was paid one week of extra wages by the government because I was over forty-five and voluntarily left the job. A strangely demoralising incentive. This marked the end of an office era for me. As personal assistant jobs began to disappear and a younger, cheaper high-tech labour force emerged, at 52 I was an ageing Girl Friday, thwarted and shooed out of the workforce.

Some of the managers organised a farewell pity party for me at the beer garden of my local pub. They presented me with a small card signed with more well wishes than I was expecting, and one ticket to the cinema.

I vowed never to work with a religious organisation ever again, no matter how desperate I was for money. Like a rat stuck in a maze, I was still focused on finding one last job. It was a financial imperative for me to work, and it was also all I had ever known. Economically, it was just too soon for me to retire.

Sometimes walking away from a job is your only option. But don't forget to give them your honest feedback as the door hits you on the way out. All I know for sure is that I would rather be unemployed than working back there. It became crystal clear that management didn't give a fat rat's arse about me. All they cared about was me getting the work done, to make them look good. I realised that my bosses enjoyed exploiting me, and the more I did, the more they expected of me, which is what my mum warned me about all those years ago. I also learnt something important about myself: that no matter what the future holds, it was in my best interest to call it quits.

At work, we have a duty of care for ourselves and each other. People are not machines. We don't adhere to empty messages on chipped coffee mugs like, 'Keep calm and carry on'. I won't follow the sage advice of numbskulls who believe that 'the universe will provide'. I worked in the school of astrophysics, and I know for a scientific fact that the universe doesn't give a toss about us. We don't matter to the stars.

It's our work friends that matter, who we spend more time with than our families and who form some of our strongest, lifelong relationships. Our collective power matters. Our compassion matters. How we treat each other at work is what matters most.

Without alliances with my colleagues and back-up from my dearest workmates who became my friends, I wouldn't have stayed in most of the jobs I had. Friendship is one of the best things about working. Workers are thrown together as strangers, busy keeping our lives afloat, glad to have a wage. Slowly, we reveal ourselves during coffee and lunch breaks, we open up over after-hours drinks. We cry together in the toilets and comfort each other. We ride out global economic crises, illness and the threat of job loss. We stick together and stick up for each other. I would have been lost without my gal pals, comrades, and mates, who are still my dear friends four decades later. The laughter and the tears we shared over all those years made working life bearable, and the workplace fit for human habitation.

Back in the 1990s at the bush uni I worked for a nasty, short-arse manager. Whenever I asked him a question about an admin task, he would flare up.

'When I say jump, you say how high!'

'When you say jump, I have to ask what for so I can figure out if I need to jump or not,' I'd say, infuriating him.

How high did I need to jump to keep a job? How do we stand up for ourselves and each other on the job? How do we stay human at work? That's the challenge. It is impossible to win the battles of unreasonable hours and excessive workload on your own. If management relishes pitting workers against each other, on your own you are done for. Worker solidarity for the common good sounds like an old-fashioned socialist notion in this digital age. Late-stage capitalism is making it harder to unite in an increasingly impermanent, global working world. But there is mighty power within a collective of workers. There is heart and strength when we join a trade union. Most of all, there is safety in numbers when workers stand united to make employers listen.

As their star rises, management float above the struggles of ordinary workers. They do not go on strike. Their energy is focused on climbing the ladder, hoisting themselves up on the backs of others. Negotiating individual contracts for their personal advancement and higher pay rates for themselves. Their loyalty is rewarded by their superiors, who did exactly the same thing before them. And so it goes on.

This scramble to the top put me right off going for higher-level roles during the last years of my career. I didn't want to be in charge of anyone's future; I could barely manage my own. To have the final say over livelihoods if someone didn't meet some target or dared to talk back gave me the willies. I had copped the fallout of bad management practices, and it was only getting worse. While I was okay to continue as a support worker, I realised that I was too old for the low-level jobs, that the old office days were gone, and that the workplace was not going to change to fit me in. That I had to make a change. I chose to protect my health and wellbeing above my income. In some ways, the rotten capitalist system had won, but so had I. I had set myself free.

Prof from the welfare office had assured me via email that he would give me a good work reference when I applied for other roles. In office work, a good work reference is everything, you can't move on without one. Later on I found out from a colleague that he had been giving me terrible work references all along, and that was why I couldn't land another job. A year later I heard on the grapevine that Prof didn't get to lord it over the office much longer. He left after crossing one too many colleagues, who stood up to him and also said no. Big Boss was eventually shafted too.

Six years later, I was at a Jamaican dance hall night when I ran into one of the leaders of the management pile-on from the welfare office. I had taken a breather from the dance floor when she stood next to me at the bar.

'Where do I know you from?' she chirped.

'I don't know, I get around,' I said, bolting outside to smoke a joint with some chums.

After all that bullshit, she didn't even remember who I was.

About a year after that, I was walking up the street and saw her sitting outside a pub at lunchtime, bitching loudly to her mates about how she was being forced out of her job. I listened and smiled and slowly walked on by, my skin growing thicker with each stride. I recalled my dad's favourite saying: 'nothing lasts forever'.

CHAPTER 8

Unemployed comedian

By mid-2012 I had come full circle. I was an old, unemployed Girl Friday, not running any hardcore addictions, apart from coffee, chocolate and cigarettes. I was in good health, and glad to be single with a roof over my head. In the weeks after I finished working, I played every CD I owned, dancing to Grace Jones and The Clash around my seventies flat. I lived in my pyjamas, busting funk and punk moves to Aretha Franklin and Public Image Ltd, celebrating my newfound freedom.

When I was a little girl, my big sisters called me Jazzy because I loved to dance. Back then I wanted to grow up to be a go-go dancer in a discothèque, and to marry Ringo Starr. I also wanted to live in a block of flats, which I thought was a big mansion, along Dandenong Road. I got the flat.

When I secured a twelve-month lease on my shabby little flat in Northcote, after abandoning my house back in 1997, I stayed there for over twenty years. I put up with despot landlords, damp, cold, searing heat and no repairs. It was dilapidated and the rent kept rising. I was petrified of being priced out or kicked out. Still, I had a place to live.

When an older woman becomes jobless, it is almost impossible to secure a new rental lease. With no employer to give you a pay slip and a reference, you are stuffed. Renting a room in a share house is fine when you are young and in your prime. But later in life, a place of your own is everything. That four-room, run-down flat was my whole world.

After sleeping in most mornings, I'd skip breakfast to cook up poached eggs and avocado brunch at noon, reading the news online for hours, shouting at the idiocy on the television. Enclosed in my small lounge room with yellowing cracked walls, I'd catch sunshine from the west in the afternoon, and smoke cigarettes perched on the doorstep of my tiny balcony, where I grew pots of parsley, lavender and flowering succulents.

As the sun went down, I'd pull on tracksuit daks and a windcheater to wander around the park and over to the shops to buy cigarettes, chocolate, milk and bread, fruit, veg and eggs. I'd check the DVDs on sale to buy classic films under $10, like *On the Waterfront* and *Breakfast at Tiffany's*, and browse the bookshops on High Street for second-hand bargains.

Still, within a couple of weeks of stopping work, I fell in a heap and had trouble getting out of bed. I was afraid I'd never work again and die in poverty. I had too much time on my hands, and I spent it dwelling on my dead-end future. I realised that this was no paid holiday, this was how it was going to be every day. So much time and so little money. Fear, sadness and disconnection haunted me. Without work, I didn't know what to do with myself. My dream of not working had come true, but it wasn't quite what I had imagined.

By spring 2012, I returned to the unemployment line cradled by the social welfare safety net. It was a foreign working world I half-heartedly tried to return to in my early fifties. All newspeak and no substance. It was way too late for me to become a senior manager; I was more senior than manager. I soon discovered I was simply too old to get my foot back in the door for any job other than a junior, part-time, temporary admin role. Like many mid-life women, before I knew it, I careered towards involuntary early retirement and became unemployable.

I felt that secure place I'd worked so hard for was in jeopardy. All I ever wanted and needed was a safe, warm place in the world, a job and a couple of friends. I missed my workmates, and I really didn't know how to stop work. Like the academics, I had become institutionalised working in university offices all those years. I needed to rediscover who I really was, and to reinvent and recreate who I wanted to be living life beyond work. I'd hidden behind my professional mask for so long, it would take me years to find myself again.

My mate Beth reckons that women like us – single, childless, working class with a decent education – are expected to make our work the main focus in life. That indentured identity never suited us. I could never see myself married to a job. What a dud relationship, all take and no give, and a husband bossing me around so I can get paid? No thanks.

Workaholics are not born that way, but are created by a management style that gets us to compete with each other for approval and job security based on our output. This suits slack managers who let staff burn out only to replace them with keen, new hires who don't know what they're getting into. The pressure to perform and the ambition to progress leaves shells of humans in its wake.

As the budget bottom-line pushes workers for more, and pulls against our human rights, workers become fearful and know our place. Bosses keep workers in check with management tools like key performance indicators, productivity targets and annual performance reviews, ensuring we stay insecure and on our toes. We become less like a human worker and more like a number to crunch. The needs of workers are lost to the demands of fanciful mission statements, unrealistic goals striving for a vague excellence based on empty words full of impossible promises, and endless growth which will be the death of us all. Who are we prepared to be to keep a job?

All of us at some point will be the worker being shafted, forced to leave, maybe to never work again. This is most likely when we get sick, are incapacitated, older and female.

When you're a younger worker it's not such a big deal to change jobs. It's flexibility, it's expanding your horizons, it allows for travel and life's adventures. But before you know it, it's three casual gigs cobbled together to make up a basic wage for much longer than you ever expected. Or maybe you hang around long enough to watch your line manager crack from stress and step up to their job. You're young and free and cannot see what lies ahead. If you could, you'd be shitting yourself just like me. That work you picked up to earn money before you get your big break in your chosen field turns out to be your career.

For women heading towards sixty, staying in the workforce is a battle. Many, like me, are engine room workers, unseen and unacknowledged. As we grow older in the workforce we are of much less value, and because we carry leave entitlements we weigh heavily on budgets. If you haven't been dubbed as management material in succession planning, if you are not interested in being a boss or if you can't take being bossed around, there is always a more enthusiastic, younger model waiting in the wings. The old grey mare who ain't what she used to be is easily put out to pasture, taking years of knowledge and expertise with her. No-one will miss her. Some will be glad to see the back of the old nag.

One by one, my big sisters hit the road to unemployment and early retirement in their fifties. First, number five sister, who had managed community media projects, became unemployable. Number two sister, who managed units for the education department, was squeezed out during a restructure. Then the end came for number three sister after years in quality assurance roles. Number five sister juggles part-time jobs. Number one sister deserved a gold watch as a sales manager because she hung in and retired in her early seventies. My brother continues to work as a waiter and barista. We all started work in our early teens, and we all hoped for financial security in later life.

Just ten more years of paid full-time work into my mid-sixties would have been great, money-wise. I disconnected from the workforce at fifty-two. I'd become too old for a lower-level role, and I had refused to be over-managed and overworked. I'd had it. When you can't marry your personal, political and professional values on the job, it often ends in career divorce. Like any separation, you will end up with less money but you will gain personal power and freedom. Even if it is the last choice you have, leaving a shitty job and getting away from bully bosses can be the most liberating act of all.

In the final years of my working life, I grew to despise the new office culture, the empty mindfulness, and the overbearing, psycho-babbling bosses. Unemployed, I didn't miss the office dramas, and I didn't miss the bosses and their constant complaints. All I ever wanted was to do a good job and to get paid for it. But everything had changed. I got it, but I didn't want it. Some say that once people retire, we drop dead. It's the retirement that kills us. It's not true. It's the years of hard work that kill us.

After almost four decades in office jobs, I had been well and truly conditioned by work. I was sure I was in there somewhere, beyond being a worker, I just couldn't see myself clearly without a job. I didn't really know how I would survive, and I didn't fully know who I was. Fear of what would happen when I stopped work had kept me in jobs that were unbearable for way too long.

Sometimes I wondered, had my working self already taken over my personal self? What if I left work, who would I be? Unemployed. Unwanted. What would I do? Not much, because everyone else is at work and I've got no money. How would

I manage? Below the poverty line, waiting in the conga line at Centrelink.

None of us are fit for work. We are trained at school, then trained on the job to mould ourselves into the workforce. Bosses told us what to do as we learnt our tools and developed new skills to keep the systems operating to run the working world. We had learnt how to fit into a hierarchy. We followed codes of conduct. We conformed to the rules to house, clothe and feed ourselves. The prize shines before us, retirement, as our working life ends with a whimper.

Work informed my identity and it fed my self-worth. Let's face it, it fed me. Work was a massive part of my life and I was a bit lost when it abruptly stopped. The working world was changing fast, and I couldn't keep up with it anymore. Like many older women, I gave my labour for free and expected little in return. I sold myself short, I suppose, but there was no going back to office work for me. I had exhausted my employee persona.

I had also outgrown my patience for being bossed around by a pack of thirty-something smart-arse managers who weren't even born by the time I had started working. When I signed up to a temp job agency they asked me, in toddler voice, 'Do you know how to use email?' and 'Are you familiar with the internet?'

'Yeah, do you know how to program a computer or build an online database?' I asked them back.

The working world creates our identity. We are shaped by our work, and we give to the world through our work. Jobless and bounced out of the workforce, we count on there being no gaping holes in the welfare safety net when we land. Because we all need help sometimes. No-one is set for life. The world does not give us security. We earn it through our work, and we know it through our relationships.

Post-work, what was my worth as a human being? Where was that elusive happiness? Epicurus, the ancient Greek philosopher, reckoned the key to happiness is a useful, analysed and connected life. He reasoned that people were best able to pursue philosophy by living a self-sufficient life surrounded by friends. This sounded like a great place for me to kickstart my life.

Gradually, I grew into being the boss of my life. At first my freedom was completely foreign to me. Once I stopped celebrating and commiserating, it took ages for me to make a mental shift, to not feel impoverished, as my post-work identity slowly took shape. I slowed down. I would take a daily walk and turn it into an event. I made reading books and watching movies my full-time occupation. Between appointments at Centrelink and shopping for bargains, the months flew by. Without the demands of working five days a week, it wasn't long before I wondered how I fit all those working hours into my life.

Reinventing myself as I went along, I dropped my disgruntled work persona and searched for a post-work identity. I recalled my pre-work self at fifteen. Who did I want to be back then? Oh yes, an authoress. How the hell was I going to become that at this late stage of the game? Then I remembered all those writing courses I'd done over the years, after work and on weekends. I dug out the dusty folders full of notes, ideas and half-finished stories. Writing was an inexpensive, creative way to occupy my time.

I had all the time in the world to write, but I was afraid to start my story or even call myself a writer. I spent my jobless days reading, writing short stories, going to half-price movies, free museums and art galleries, walking around parks, eating well and sleeping like a log every night. If this was a writer's life, I supposed I could get used to it.

Weaning myself off the security of a regular wage was hard. I knew how to live without spending money; Mum had taught us well. Stay home and you don't spend any money. I ate simply and made everything last. I walked miles and went to free events. I couldn't afford to buy pot and I didn't feel the need to get stoned anymore. The after-hours numb-down of smoking weed had stopped when I left work. I had finished with the work-reward cycle and cut short my expensive habit, cultivated in response to work-based stress. I felt fit and sure of myself.

In between my half-hearted attempts to get work, I reconnected with my mates who still worked, over evening and weekend drinks for a chat and a laugh. I figured that I had made some progress coming back to life in my early fifties. Twenty family and friends celebrated my fiftieth birthday with me at a pub. It felt like I was back in the land of the living. Unlike my fortieth, when I was homeless, penniless and staying at my mum's retirement village unit, glad some siblings showed up with gifts of crockery, saucepans, cutlery and towels. Like a sad engagement party for one.

Early retirement sounds lovely, but spat out of the workforce at the tail end of my last earning years, my life was about hanging onto the money I had saved, to make it last as long as possible, and worrying constantly about the cost of everything. I couldn't get my head around not having any more income. I knew that my superannuation wouldn't last, and if I lived long enough, it definitely wouldn't.

One night I met a bright spark in her sixties at a workshop.

'So what year were you born?' she asked me.

'I was born in 1960, why do you ask?'

'Did you know, according to statistics, you will probably live until you're 105?'

'Not if I can help it. I'm smoking as fast as I can; I can't afford to live that long!'

Apart from my savings, I had little to show for almost forty years on a basic admin wage. Part of me was still shitting bricks that I'd end up living in a park out of my shopping jeep in my leather coat, lining up at soup kitchens. I knew for sure I wasn't going to make it to 105 without another job.

My friends and family also worried about when I would find work. I was not ready to retire at fifty-two; it was a shock to my system to have so much time, and money-wise it was ten years too soon. I had been conditioned to work. Like a confused Pavlov's dog waiting for the bell to ring, I was a salivating mess with no rewards. My financial future seemed impossible.

Also, I couldn't get my hands on my super savings until I turned fifty-five. I waited, and wore three more years of mounting debt.

At Centrelink's insistence, I became stuck in a loop of compulsive thinking about finding another job. Finding a new job is a bit like finding a new man. You check out the ones available that best fit your values and experience, apply and wait for a response. Then you go for a meeting to see if you want to offer each other the position. Depending on what you can put up with, you may live happily ever after, or decline the offer and quit. The trouble was, the older I got the less I could put up with, from a man or a job.

As we grow older, women fade from view. By my fifties I was generally being ignored in public, which suited me. Having discovered my cloak of invisibility, I took full advantage of it. I'd steal avocados, pricing them as potatoes at the self-serve check-out. I'd stuff cold meat, cheese and Belgian chocolates into the pockets of my leather coat. No-one noticed.

One day standing in the queue at the Aldi check-out, a tanned, twenty-ish hipster dude with white man dreads stood in front of me and said to the older European woman working the register, 'Won't it be great when you leave this job? You can do whatever you want!' She looked up blankly, dark circles under her eyes, shook her head and continued to swipe his groceries. Dread dude had no idea what an older woman faced being out of work. Her reality was invisible to him.

Like the thirty-ish tall guy in a business suit on the tram one day. Tram man stood by the doors hanging onto the upper rails with his armpit directly over my head, talking loudly on his phone. When I asked him to give me some room, he claimed he didn't see me. Yeah, I know, I'm invisible!

Enduring months of unemployment, I stopped slapping on make-up every day. One morning I caught myself in the mirror. Moon face cheeks sunken from missing back teeth, breath pungent from a gum abscess, and tongue coated white. Deep parallel frown lines between my eyebrows, skin pigmentation and pockmarks complimented my thick glasses, correcting a turn in my bung right eye. On closer inspection, hazel irises swam in bloodshot whites, and a large floater blocked my view. I ran my fingers through short, spikey brassy-blonde hair, thinning and with grey roots. There I stood, five foot nothing, round shoulders, with a middle-aged spread from too much toast and pasta. After working in offices for nearly four decades, I had turned into a bit of a monster.

For many years post-treatment, my skin would erupt in red, weeping sores. The eczema had spread to my face, and it caused me great distress. At a make-up selling party one evening after work, a dozen women and I had spent hundreds of dollars each on a range of skin care and make-up, including products to cover up and products to remove the stuff.

The next morning, I used six products to create my smooth new face for the office. It took half an hour to apply the layers and I was late for work. I was flattered when the women at work noticed and asked, 'What is your secret?' and 'Have you met someone?' The men said, 'You look attractive, now.' Soon, I wouldn't go outside without my mask of make-up. It was costing me a small fortune.

My mate Beth told me that one day she didn't wear mascara to work and a female colleague asked her, 'Are you okay?' It wasn't R U OK day.

We wear our lives on our faces. Every smile, scowl and trauma map out our journey. Lines and scars that cannot be erased. We hide our imperfections from the world, and cover up what lurks beneath the surface. We display pretty facades to get a job and to keep a job. With a splash of blush and ruby lips, we hide our illnesses, humanness, our flaws and our age. We disguise our vulnerabilities. We put on a brave face, and we can't wait to wipe it all off when we get home.

Now I examined my creased face, reflected for the first time in decades, unmade and fed up. I realised that I had lived in the service of others, stressed out of my head for way too long. It had taken its toll, and I was a bit of a wreck. I felt useless, unwanted, and unrecognisable. I chucked myself in the shower, cleansed my skin, covered up the spots, dried my hair and put on clean clothes. I stood up straight to face my reflection and cracked a grin. I had scrubbed up all right. I hadn't lost my smile.

On a good day, the world was my oyster. I was secretly excited about how I could live my life any way I wanted. On a bad day, I worried about every shitty interaction and how the hell I was going to get back to work and put on that persona again. Despite my nagging fears, I felt stronger and happier than I had in years. Six months after leaving that last toxic workplace, my neck and shoulder pain was gone. I managed to get by living on the cheap, just like when I was growing up.

I knew that the longer I was out of the workforce the harder it would be to get back in. I felt oddly ashamed for being unemployed for so long, a non-productive member of society. I didn't like being dependent on the government, who could cut me off at any time. Like a rat with OCD, I continued to search for work near home. I wanted less hours, a supportive team of equals, and decent pay. But my fantasy job did not exist.

Melbourne's mid-winter bone-chiller wind and rain swept me back to Preston Centrelink. I bolted past the Indian eyebrow-threading salons, shisha cafes and French-Vietnamese pastry shops, into a beige building across from the Woolies car park. I joined the winding queue inside the open-plan office and clocked a new sign at the counter: 'Abuse of staff will not be tolerated.'

A short, nuggetty bloke around fifty stood behind me in white overalls and whispered over my shoulder, 'I'm a house painter, just moved back to Melbourne after ten years away. I can't use a computer.'

'Just tell them and they'll help you. Good luck.' He was going to need it.

I took a seat in the rows of dank, green armchairs in the holding lounge, sitting with twenty soaked customers. The smell of wet socks wafted my way, and the pissy stink of damp raincoats hung in the air. A sluggish security guard stood beside a CCTV camera, crooking his neck at the wall-mounted television. 'You'll never live to regret it,' blared a hyped-up man on an ad for a glamour photo shoot.

A keen Indian couple moved me along so they could use the computer to scroll through IT positions. I sat near two old Greek fellas shouting at each other like they were at their local club. Next to me was a woman like me, redundant, in an off-white collar under a jacket with sagging shoulder pads, checking her wristwatch. Next to us was an elderly Vietnamese mother and middle-aged daughter, listening for their name to be called out and mispronounced.

A family of chunky, white sisters gabbled around a laminate table, handing a rattle to a dribbling baby in a pram. An African Muslim teenager in a pink headscarf leaned on a column checking her phone. Mid-forties tradesmen shifted impatiently, arms crossed above their tool belts, keeping an eye on the agitated, skinny men with neck-tattoos loudly scheming their next score into a phone. A First Nations woman in a blue hoodie circled the room then disappeared, as three cops strode in searching for someone. When they left, the room exhaled.

A veteran dude in his sixties marched into the fray in ragged jeans and a faded khaki T-shirt, approaching the counter ready for action.

'303 691 735 C,' he said to the twenty-ish female Centrelink officer.

'Hello, how can I help you?'

'303 691 735 C, that's my number. You need to pay me the money I'm owed. It was supposed to be in the bank last week, look it up!'

'Sir, there is no need to speak to me like that.'

'303 691 735 C. That's my number, look me up!'

Meanwhile, a smiling African man in his forties who had finished his appointment turned to the room with two thumbs up, singing, 'I don't have to be at Centrelink anymore today!', and danced towards the exit.

We waited, and waited, and waited, sharing the shame of being on the bones of our arse and afraid that the social welfare safety net may give way at any minute. I had been living off my final wage and leave pay for two months. Now that was gone, I was desperate, and eligible for the dole, or so I thought.

After an hour, I was called in for an interview with a short, rotund woman around my age, ankles bulging over her flats. Voula was sorry.

'You will have to wait twelve weeks for a payment, because you left your job. And the first payment will only be one week.'

'WHAT?'

'You left your job. You have to wait. And you need to prove to us you are not sub-letting your flat. You have to provide us with a copy of your lease.'

'Voula, I have lived in my one-bedroom rental flat for over fifteen years on an expired lease. If I ask for a new lease, my landlord will put up the rent. Trust me, Voula, Centrelink have taken my word for years. There is no reason for you to think I'm lying now.'

Voula agreed to sign me up for the unemployment benefit, after I provided them with a copy of the latest rent increase letter. The government rules were getting much tougher. I had to put my rent, bills and food on my credit card. I withdrew cash from my credit card to make the monthly repayment. I hardly surfaced for fear of spending money while I waited three long months for that one-week payment.

The following week I went for a job interview back at the bush university. It was a research and admin position in the strategic projects area of the Vice-Chancellor's office. It was part-time, casual, fixed-term and it hadn't been advertised. My dear friend Duck, who I worked with at the bush uni years earlier, put me onto it. They wanted a post-graduate, but I went for it anyway. It was twenty hours a week to research and write ministerial briefs, prepare speeches and manage events. It was way too much work for the pay rate, for those hours and for one person.

To get a look-in, I had to prepare a briefing paper, a mock funding bid to support the university's wildlife reserves. I relished writing the paper, remembering how I'd helped save the reserves twenty years earlier with my old mate Jorge. I whipped up the application in five hours, put it in, and landed an interview. On my way to the bush uni, I travelled on the bus past my old street, where I'd left my doomed house behind, and where three new units had been built.

I entered the student admin building where I worked back in the nineties, taking the stairs up to the V-C offices on the top floor. I sat on the same old Chesterfield sofa, and noticed the new slate grey carpet tiles. Marlene the manager, six feet tall, pushing fifty, bounded towards me. Without a word, she glared down at me then turned and went into a room. I assumed she wanted me to follow her. Before I sat down, she had asked me the first question.

'What makes you think you'd be suitable for this position?'

By the time I finished my answer, Marlene reckoned I had answered all of her questions.

'Your written piece was quirky, but unusable,' she said.

She was clearly not keen on me, and the feeling was mutual. The Chief Operations Officer burst into the room.

'I thought you needed to be off campus,' Marlene snapped.

'No, no, I'm here now, let's move on,' he said, and sat down to skim my application.

Marlene was unimpressed.

'So, Kristine, you worked with the university some time ago I see. Tell me what you've been up to since then?' said the COO.

He then interrupted me mid-sentence to take a phone call, and bolted out the door saying he had to meet the Minister. I found out later a post-graduate got the job.

I continued to ask everyone I knew who was working about any jobs coming up. But the longer I was out of work, the more unemployable I became. I told myself that money would come, and all the self-help books and horoscopes told me the same. I just needed to stay positive, live into my dreams, and be grateful. Instead of believing that complete load of hocus-pocus, I prayed to the Centrelink goddess that my fortnightly payment was on its way, and checked my negative bank balance and rising credit card debt every day.

Centrelink's rules required me to trawl through a sea of online job ads. I couldn't tell if they were real jobs or fake jobs. Some were looking for sex workers and some were looking for slaves. 'Must be available on call 24/7', 'exciting and stimulating career opportunity', and 'be the boss of your clients'. Reading six-page position descriptions for the 'ideal role in a high-energy crew' made my stomach churn. If the job ad said anything like, 'fun team vibe', 'must hit the ground running' or 'is happy to work under pressure', I was out. I would apply for ten jobs a week and get no replies, which was better than ten rejection emails.

As full-time, ongoing employment became scarcer for old ducks like me, I noticed an influx of online advertisements for self-starter business opportunities. Multi-level marketing was thriving. 'Be your own boss, own your own business, turn friends, family, colleagues into customers, make a profit, win-win!' These pyramid selling schemes involved throwing a drunk shopping party for your lonely unemployed girlfriends and broke single mums busting for social contact. The product party host would flog overpriced candles, costume jewellery or skin care in their home. Re-ordering was set up online in perpetuity, auto-shipping forever. I had also heard about Botox injection parties, popular among ageing, enterprising females. Perfect for snapping that online profile picture. Making money from your broke mates was not my cup of tea.

I landed a full-time, one-month contract data-entry gig through the temp agency. For $17.50 an hour, I logged donations for the Guide Dogs, where the dogs were treated better than me. My colleagues would enter the office each morning with a chirpy 'good morning', crouching down to pat a dozing labrador laying on the floor under my desk and ignoring me completely.

At the same time, the bathroom of my old Northcote rental flat was undergoing major repairs after years of neglect. I had reported water leaking from pipes into the damp walls for years, but the miserly landlord had refused to fix it. I had to decamp to my mum's unit for six weeks. To get to work I travelled on a tram from Reservoir, then a bus, then a half-hour walk to Kew. A three-hour round trip through rain, wind and hail. Centrelink rewarded me with accrued working credits, so I got to keep my full unemployment payment and my wages. Because my flat was uninhabitable during the renovations, I requested a rent refund and got that too. For a few weeks, I felt rich.

When the temporary work was over, I was assigned a new job network case manager, Mindy, who was Indian-Australian, maybe twenty. She rang me one summer day with an exciting job opportunity.

'I found an administration role for you. It is part-time, a one-year contract, at a meat retailer.'

'A meat retailer, what's that?'

'I think it may be where they sell meat? It is on your train line. It is in Mernda.'

'Oh, I think it might be a butcher shop. An hour away from my place.'

'Yes, you would be highly suitable for the position. You would be their bookkeeper. They are willing to pay you $15 an hour. It is for twenty hours a week. Would you like me to send you to the job?'

'Thanks Mindy, I'll have to get back to you.'

I burst into tears.

At my next appointment I explained my precarious financial situation to Mindy.

'About that meat retailer job, thank you Mindy. But it would only pay me $300 a week, minus 30 per cent tax – say $210 a week in my hand. That would not even cover my rent, and I would lose my rent assistance. I would not have a travel or health care concession. I'd be working for much less than the dole. I'm not sure it is worth my while to apply. What do you think?'

'I understand. It is not easy, is it?'

'No, it is not.'

Mindy would have copped flak from her boss for not pushing me into that job, because that's how the private job networks get funding from the government. When an unemployed client lands ongoing work, the job network provider gets paid $6000. Mindy got to keep her job if I got a job. At our fortnightly appointments, we barely spoke and she signed off the necessary forms. Mindy had a heart.

After I left the workforce, I looked back on how many evenings and weekends I had wasted bitching with friends about how shit my job was and how crazy my managers were. I had wasted too much of my spare time not having fun. Now that I wasn't working anymore, this was going to change. By late summer 2013, I made a decision. To find some fun.

I enrolled in a comedy movement workshop led by a kooky Hungarian hypnotist. We met before the class, on a sunny Sunday afternoon in the back blocks of Southbank, Melbourne. I wore sunglasses, and made sure I didn't look deeply into his eyes. He told me the next two hours would change my life. I wanted to believe him.

In a circle of six people, we said who we are and what we wanted from the workshop. 'I'm unemployed and funny. I want to have fun and make people laugh, and maybe make some money out of it,' I said. The hypnotist asked us to walk, clap and recite a favourite poem. Mine was taught to me by my dead, funny father. 'The boy stood on the burning deck, picking his nose like mad, rolling it up in little balls, and throwing it at his dad.' Everyone cracked up. It was exciting to make people laugh on purpose. I realised that I hadn't laughed so hard in a long time.

A few weeks later I got an email from the broken ballerina who had organised the workshop. She invited me to join her comedy writing incubator group. 'There'll be cupcakes,' she said, so I went along. There wasn't much comedy writing but it was good to be with the group from the workshop again.

The next morning there was an email thanking me for coming. However, due to my 'rugged individualism', she suggested it would be better that I didn't come back, and maybe I should start my own writing group. I replied that I was happy to take my 'rugged individualism' and explore it elsewhere. As the late, great Groucho Marx said, 'Please accept my resignation. I don't want to belong to any club that would accept someone like me as a member.'

Six months later, after learning the ropes from watching stand-up comedians at open mic nights in bar basements and the back rooms of pubs, I got my first spot. My debut open mic performance was in a run-down Irish pub at the end of a Melbourne cobblestone laneway on a wet Monday night. As it pissed down rain, water streamed through holes in the roof above the stage, soaking the male comedian who was up before me.

On stage, with the spotlight blinding me, from what I could tell my first five minutes of live comedy was jaw-dropping. All I could make out was a row of open mouths. I couldn't tell if the mainly young adult male audience were laughing or if they were gobsmacked. I'd gone deaf with stage fright.

Afterwards my two mates, who came along for support, told me that I did get some laughs. As an older female budding comedian, I had stunned the crowd into bursts of embarrassed laughter with my brash, shock-value material, which needed some work. For the first time in my adult life, I was free to be my comedic self with no fear of being sacked or banned. I loved every belly laugh, giggle and gaffe. I became a volunteer comedian.

In between Centrelink appointments, shopping and stories, I became an old, unemployed woman with a lot of time on my hands thinking, so what do I do now? It really didn't feel like it was my right to stop working completely. I felt like I still owed my labour to the world. But the working world had no place for me in it. Only short-term, part-time contracts or gig work that paid less than the dole. It was the scrap heap for me. Over time I grew to love my new worthless life.

Part of the deal with Centrelink payments was mega mutual obligations, outlined in a signed job activity plan. This involved face-to-face sessions with a Job Network case manager to look for jobs that weren't there. At my weekly appointment with my case manager, late-twenties Mark suggested I should get a sugar daddy.

'You mean a sugar granddaddy don't you Mark?' I replied.

He laughed at my gag and I smiled politely. I told Mark that I was bullied out of my office profession.

'Don't worry, I have another six women your age on the books and the same thing happened to them. Just dumb yourself down Kristine, you are way too professional. There's a call centre job going, or data entry for $15 an hour with the government. They'll give you a job, unless you're a bitch or a thief.'

'What if I'm both?'

We had a good old laugh while Mark ticked his boxes and told me he was leaving, as he had found a better job.

My next case manager was Jurgen, a newly arrived German in his mid-thirties. At one appointment he asked me, 'So who is your hero?' I didn't have one. He suggested Angela Merkel.

'Oh, you mean *Time* magazine Woman of the Year, Germany's Chancellor?'

'Yes, Kristine.'

'Okay. How about I do a Certificate III in ruling a European nation, and maybe for homework, I can invade Poland?'

Jurgen laughed.

At my next appointment, I confessed my dream of becoming a writer. To my surprise, Jurgen granted me a couple of hundred dollars retraining money to participate in a women's comedy workshop and a writing course. He also swung me money for new 'office' clothes that I bought at Target. Jurgen and I both knew there were no paid jobs for writers or comedians on the corkboard. But as Kurt Vonnegut once said, 'The arts are not a way to make a living. They are a very human way of making life more bearable.'

Each week Jurgen and I would meet and I'd tell him my latest gags.

'Jurgen, did you know Centrelink offered me a job?'

'Is this one of your jokes Kristine?'

'No, true story Jurgen. They want me to do part-time data entry for $15 an hour.'

'That's wonderful, when do you start?'

'I told them thank you for the generous offer, but I would rather be giving hand-shandies to drunks.'

'Oh no, you didn't, that's so funny, you got me again Kristine. What is hand-shandies?'

'Never mind Jurgen, let's just say it is the only job where I'd be getting equal pay with men.'

I found my voice doing stand-up comedy. I learnt how to write and perform sets, and connected to a funny women's community, challenging the male order with our shenanigans. Men dominated the comedy scene with dick jokes and mum jokes, which made the male audiences laugh, and the women wince. They say whatever your gags are about is what you are about.

I'd gussy up to perform on stage, blonde hair spiked with product, blushed cheeks, raised eyebrows, heavy mascara, and red lippy to focus the audience on my mouthful of material. I'd dust off my best work suits and sparkly shirts to put on a show. My expressive rubber-face served my comedy well. I'd impersonate creepy old men puckering up for a kiss, and break into my sharpie dance if all else failed. For a cheap, easy laugh, I'd mention that I was either wearing the highest waisted trousers in the room, or I had the lowest hanging tits. I'd do absurdist bits about right-wing politicians, getting banned, women's liberation, disappointing love, hipsters, technology and home appliances, ageing, unemployment and office work.

'Ever done one of those Myer-Briggs personality tests at work? You answer some psycho questions for the boss to find out what type of office animal they've employed. I lied on mine, yeah, just like I lied to get the job. See, when I started office work in the seventies no-one was into all these thinky-feely assessment tools. Back then bosses wanted a "do your job and shut the fuck up" type personality. Turns out the test reckoned I'm an I-I-J-L-B. An Intuitive, Introverted, Judgemental, Lying Bitch. That's what forty years of office work will do to you.'

I performed comedy festival shows at Melbourne and Adelaide Fringe, and spent two years running an equal-opportunity open mic comedy night at a local bar. I would book the acts, promote the gigs on social media, and run up and down the length of High Street sticky-taping posters to lampposts. I took the same approach to my comedy as I had to my office work: I promised myself that I'd give it my all for as long as I enjoyed it.

Through comedy I found a new source of post-work stress to keep me on my toes, and a new ratbag community to belong to.

Sometimes the gags would land and sometimes not; that was the process to find the funny. But I never got to grips with the piercing attention on stage – some punters told me I was funnier off-stage.

It was a fun but costly pursuit. There were festival show fees, travel and accommodation costs, and beers with comedians. I noticed that the comedy scene was light on working-class performers. Most of the comedians who hung in year after year were funny enough, and could afford to chase their dream long-term.

I called it quits on comedy six months before my dear comedy sister, Eurydice, was stalked and murdered walking home from a gig. Eurydice had often done spots at my comedy room and we had performed at Adelaide Fringe together. She was funny and fearless.

Spilling my guts on stage to a pack of random, drunk men had begun to feel unsafe. It was risky travelling around on public transport late at night, walking the streets to and from gigs chasing laughs. After Eurydice's death there were no laughs left in the comedy scene for me. I consoled myself imagining her in comedy room heaven, where everyone was laughing together. Where there were no dickheads telling dick jokes, and no men hating on women for a laugh.

While I loved writing comedy sets, the highs and lows of performing were too much for me. The beer and late nights also took their toll. Frankly, I'd left my run a bit late. After giving comedy a good crack for five years, I had said it all and had a ball. I had liberated my sense of humour, and I had learnt how to lighten up the darkest moments with humour. I had also discovered that I preferred the page to the stage.

CHAPTER 9

Volunteering for the dole

IN FEBRUARY 2015, on the day I turned fifty-five, I headed up to Preston Centrelink with a spring in my step. After three years of living on my credit card and loans, I had come of age. Instead of attending torturous job network appointments, I could fulfil Centrelink's mutual obligations by volunteering with a not-for-profit organisation. On that momentous birthday, I officially 'retired', according to the superannuation people. I was allowed to draw down $25,000 to pay off my debts, a great relief. I also set up a small income stream to top up a meagre unemployment allowance.

On that wonderful day, my Centrelink goddess was Sharon, who was also retiring after thirty years on the job. Our smiles didn't fade for a second as we chatted about our post-work plans and how we would spend our free time. Sharon was into embroidery and gardening, and I was into writing and music.

We filled in all the forms, ticking all the boxes for my transition from dole bludger to volunteer.

I had already been volunteering for two years as a receptionist with a community radio station in Collingwood. I helped out as an old Girl Friday (and Thursday), sitting on the front desk a couple of days a week, answering the phone, greeting musicians and assisting program announcers and staff. Once a year the radio station would pay me for a few weeks work to fill-in part-time for the office manager when she took leave. It wasn't worth my while financially to do the part-time paid work, because when I declared the income, they deducted money from my unemployment allowance. But I did it anyway, because I wanted to support my new friend, the office manager, who had supported me as a new volunteer. It also kept Centrelink off my back.

Volunteering was much more rewarding than paid work. It restored my dignity. Instead of being forced to look for jobs that paid peanuts, that I didn't want or couldn't get, I felt needed and useful again, and I didn't have to get too involved with workplace dramas. I felt valued and connected as the front-of-house fringe-dweller.

Financially and psychologically, I was much better off on the dole volunteering than working part-time for minimum wage. Volunteer work gave me a chance to make a valued contribution. There is no money exchanged, just an exchange of time, energy, ideas and knowledge. It connected me to the wider world and it gave me hope. It restored my self-worth and shifted my focus outwards, beyond my four walls.

My social life also picked up in the local community radio scene. Sometimes I got given free tickets to local live music events. Plus, it fulfilled my Centrelink obligations, and that meant I could pay my rent.

Post-work, my greatest source of stress and aggravation was dealing with Centrelink. I wrestled with their self-serve computerised systems, and with wrangling Centrelink staff face-to-face and over the phone. Anyone on government support payments knows exactly what I'm talking about. That sick pit in your stomach during contact, that feeling of rising mutual distrust.

Before every Centrelink appointment I attended or call I made, I would say an affirmation: 'Let me help you to help me.' This reminded me that there was another human being behind the counter or on the other end of the phone. A worker just like I used to be. Someone who was also hanging onto their job. Someone who needed to keep a roof over their head too.

It was always a punishing wait on the phone, hoping for a Centrelink call centre worker to pick up. An hour or more, listening to wobbly recordings of muzak that I could have learnt to play by ear if I had a piano. Then a click, your heart skips a beat for a split-second, thinking, praying that a human has answered your call. Only to hear again their pre-recorded message about being honest and courteous and redirecting you to their website. If you don't want to wait anymore, someone will call you back.

Yeah, sure. I don't want to wait, but I've waited this long, I can't hang up now.

Sometimes I would act out my old-lady script and explain how I couldn't figure out their online systems, because I really couldn't, but it was all my fault because I was a silly billy. Can you help me please? This suited the younger Centrelink workers, keen to prove their superior IT skills. At other times I would cry, genuinely, because I wasn't going to make my rent and I would be put out on the street, and I wasn't getting off the line until they sorted out my payment, help me *please!* This worked if they did not want a too-hard basket-case escalated up to their manager. At other times the payment problem would be too difficult even for the call centre worker, so they'd tell me to go into a Centrelink office. Shuddering at their suggestion, it was clear resistance was futile.

In-person Centrelink appointments are the worst. I'd plan my outfit the night before, dressing down for success. A white-collar work shirt, plain waisted black trousers and a beige trench coat, paid for by Centrelink. Black-and-white checked sneakers to remind them I wasn't that well-off and I was not staying long. Not too dressed up or I would look like I ought to be in a job. Not too dressed down or I would look like a professional dole bludger.

Even with an appointment, I'd wait for over an hour to see someone if it was a busy day. Waiting for my turn, I always felt like something was about to go horribly wrong, even as a legitimate volunteer. The Centrelink officer may be shitty and ready to turn, maybe apply a new ruling, an on-the-spot reassessment, wielding an underlying threat to cut off my payment.

The trick was to submit to their bureaucratic will. Leave them no room for doubt with lots of intense eye contact – a little crazy goes a long way. Hypnotise them into thinking that you are a trusted un-employee. Now you are unemployed, you are in fact working for Centrelink. You are doing their job with them. You are one of them. You are happy to help.

It's best to take notes and make a copy of every form for your own file because they lose stuff. Look up their regulations and rules online, and ask them questions, lots of questions. Because they won't tell you much at all. This is one of the ways governments keep the unemployment numbers down: making it as difficult as possible for people to sign on. I would wear them down with pity and requests for more information. Centrelink's philosophy towards their jobless clients comes from a place of mistrust and disdain. And they wonder why we feel the same.

One day I headed into my local inner-city Centrelink office to lodge my annual volunteer agreement form. The Centrelink officer at the counter, Robo-Karen, a stony-faced woman in her forties, scanned me up and down like I was a barcode.

'What's your number?' she said.

I told her my customer reference number and asked her for an appointment.

'You can use the app for that. Don't you have the app? Have you got a mobile phone?'

'Yes, but I don't use the app, my phone is old. I would like to see someone, please.'

'You are disadvantaging yourself, you know. In future, you will have to use the app.'

'Can I please just see someone to help me lodge these forms?'

'You know you're wasting your own time. You'll have to wait.'

'Yes, I know. I have plenty of time and I'm happy to wait.'

I took a seat near the only other old duck in the waiting area.

Robo-Karen was my sister factotum, and I knew exactly what she was thinking. 'How come I have to work in this shitty job and she doesn't even go to work?' In the future, she will be out of a job too, waiting on the other side of the counter, just like me.

Mum was heading towards ninety, getting older and sicker. As the youngest daughter, unemployed and living nearby, I was pegged to look after her. Fortunately, I had plenty of time to keep an eye on her changing needs, and I was glad to spend her last few years close to her. I learnt a lot about the decline into old age, a real eye-opener for both of us. I felt useful caring for her as she had done for me. Caring was another kind of volunteer work I performed out of love.

Mum also showed me how to fill my days pottering around when the busyness of work life is over. Reading the news, doing crosswords, having a chat about the crazy state of the world, and what to eat. The stories she repeated revealed life lessons that stuck with me: the more you give, the more they'll take, don't let the bastards drag you down, and make your own little place in the world.

The working world had changed so much since she had retired in 1990, it was hard for her to understand why I couldn't get another good job. I'd explain how I was only getting offered low-paid, part-time contracts that weren't worth going off the dole for. She did understand this, and how easily women are shunted out of the workforce as we age.

I did whatever I could over the years to support and comfort her, and keep her company. Coffee and cake in Preston after medical appointments. Trips to the shops and the local library, until she couldn't walk up the street anymore.

When Mum turned fifty, she had put out an all-points bulletin to her adult offspring. 'Don't call me Mum anymore. If I hear the word "mum" one more time, I'm going to scream! You all need to start calling me by my name, Laurel.' Her job was done, but she'd always be our mum.

Laurel's straight silver hair was cut short and her sharp hazel eyes, just like mine, didn't miss a trick. Due to a degeneration of her spine, she had shrunk a few inches over the decades, which we avoided mentioning, except when her great grandkids visited and stood back-to-back with granny Laurel and she'd say how tall they'd grown.

On Saturdays, Laurel and I would go shopping at the supermarket and sometimes call into the TAB pokies place for lunch. We hated the pokies. We had both worked too hard for our money to pump it into a thieving machine. But the food was cheap and the portions generous. We'd eat and watch the mesmerised players, noticing that on a win, the pokies machine played a digital version of 'Hallelujah!', an old church favourite.

We'd discuss the news, TV, books, politics and people. Laurel would often drop a sharp observation out of the corner of her mouth about one of her neighbours from the village sitting a few tables away. She'd whisper a biting comment or update me on their latest family tragedy.

Conversations with Laurel were always worldly and wonderful.

'What books are you reading at the moment, Laurel?'

'Well, I got that Sartre out of the library. I didn't really take to his way of thinking. I think he was a bit of a wanker. I bet he wasn't slaving his guts out in a factory and looking after seven kids. He wouldn't have had time for all that thinking then, would he?'

'No, he wouldn't, Laurel.'

'All those men, they don't know how good they've got it. They don't know what they're doing, and we don't know the half of what they get up to. It's the rotten capitalist system, it favours the rich and punishes the poor, that's what it has always been about. The little woman is supposed to stay home and look after the kids, and the men go to work or go away to war. What's it all for?'

'You're right, Laurel, it makes no sense at all.'

Cleaning out her kitchen cupboards we'd share a laugh over half-full jars and packets of dried food years past the use-by date. I helped her as best as I could, especially when she was sick or losing her appetite, cleaning up after occasional accidents and promising not to tell. Eventually she let the marvellous women from the local council home help services in, just to vacuum and dust.

I'd stay overnight and we'd eat her meals-on-wheels and play 'guess what the brown stuff in the foil tray is', watching *Wheel of Fortune* on TV. At sundown and over at the shops, sometimes she got aggressive, like the bad old days. I saw the signs of dementia gradually take her over.

When her mobility declined, Laurel was no longer the boss of her life. After a fall walking up to the shops one day, she could get into the bath, but couldn't get out, and that changed everything. She bit her nails to the quick, silently freaking out about her loss of independence. I stopped getting annoyed at her goodbye tagline, 'take care', because I knew what she was really saying was, take care of yourself love, because I'll be going soon.

She was adept at hiding her slow downhill slide. Over the phone she sounded good as gold. But in reality, she needed much more help than we could give her and she was brave enough to admit it.

One day when I was visiting, she said, 'If I won TattsLotto, I would go into aged care tomorrow. I am really feeling it in my body, Kris. You don't know what it's like getting old. It's scary, you feel vulnerable. I don't know what's going to happen, stuck here on my own.'

'I hear you Laurel, let's look into it.'

Laurel had already started trying to convince me to move into her tiny spare room to be her full-time carer. She had it all figured out.

'It'd be a great help to me. You could be like those ladies from the home help service. You could get the carers pension, move in here and look after me. You're so kind Kristine, you'd be really good at that sort of thing.'

'But I don't want to do that. I don't mean to be rude Laurel, but I don't want to live in a retirement village with really old people. Besides, what would happen to me when you go into care? Where would I live when you have to sell your unit to pay for the aged care place?'

'Oh, I never thought of that.'

That was a hard conversation to have, but it was the truth.

I asked her if she'd like me to ring up an aged care place to arrange a visit. 'Yes, that'd be good love. Because I was talking to Gwen up Northland bus stop last week. You remember her, she's the one with the four grandkids and her daughter had to leave her horrible husband because he was bashing her, and they had to move into Gwen's place? Anyway, Gwen's gone into care and she reckons it's alright. As long as I don't have to put up with any stupid, old bastard men, and it doesn't cost too much, it might be alright for me too.'

Starting at the low-cost end, number one sister and I arranged for Laurel to visit an aged care home in Bundoora. We called it Twin Peaks. The stink of urine on the khaki linoleum floor got right up our noses. An elderly woman with bleach-blonde ringlets in a T-shirt with 'heartbreaker' across her chest pushed past us in a wheelchair, her pink leg-stump poking out beneath a short, pleated skirt. Wonky men and bent-over women in varying states of decay wandered around, wondering who and where they were. We were not impressed.

The aged care place Laurel eventually chose looked after her like she was their own mother. After a couple of strokes, they moved her to a high-care room. Regular morphine doses numbed her end-of-life discomfort and softened her timely departure. Mum clocked off at ninety years of age in April 2018.

Laurel reckoned that the trouble is, you don't know what it's going to be like in old age until you get there. She spoke less and less as she drifted into her last years; the fire in her belly was going out. But she was a wise, tough woman who passed her bitter-sweet understanding of the world on to us. Having a job was everything to our mother. She'd say 'money can be your best friend,' and she was right in many ways. The love she mustered was miraculous, starting her life as an orphaned child, working her guts out in factory jobs to support her seven children. Divorcing in an era when women just didn't. She was one of the hardest working women I knew. She inspired me to keep going no matter what. Laurel was a legend in her own lounge room and I miss her.

At fifty-five I faced the fact that I was all washed-up, career-wise. Fortunate and poor, my super savings and the dole kept me going. Life on the dole is life on the cheap. Living close to friends, family, maintaining community connections, and affordable, secure housing near shops and transport was all that mattered. I lived simply and well. This helped me to focus on reading, writing and looking forward to a future that I had worked hard for. A future, if I'm careful with my savings, that I can maybe afford with ongoing government support. If I can just keep jumping through Centrelink's hoops for the rest of my life, I can cover the cost of my housing, and eat the rest of my savings. Adaptation and resilience are my strengths, won through hardship.

Looking back, I was fortunate to have been born in a pre-digital era that gave me forty years of ongoing, salaried jobs plus superannuation savings. My decent working conditions and wages had been hard won by trade union members. The big difference in the twenty-first century is how many workers feel completely alone.

Out of the workforce, I had time to question everything about being in and out of work. Like, how come millions of dollars of government funds go to those job network providers to tell me that I should dumb myself down, wear more make-up and work for peanuts? Why are jobs that are mainly occupied by women, like admin, caring, cleaning, nursing and teaching jobs, still the lowest-paid roles across the world? It makes no sense. Without us essential women workers, the world would be completely out of control. We'd all be disorganised, filthy, neglected, sick, stupid or dead. Add a swarm of robots and artificial intelligence into the new century workforce mix, and some foresee a future devoid of women workers entirely.

Throughout 2012 while I was working for the Christians, trade union members employed across the social welfare sector petitioned our female prime minister, Julia Gillard, to raise the basic award wage for community services workers. We sent the PM thousands of purple postcards imprinted with a pair of big red lips and a message that read, 'Send a kiss to Julia'. She responded, and social and community services workers were paid more, at a starting rate of $21 per hour. It was still not enough for the arse-wiping, life-giving and death-defying duties performed while caring for our communities, but it was a good start.

It was a just reward for the workers providing child care so women could stay in the workforce, and for those who gave respite and full-time care to elderly relatives or family members with disabilities. Surely these human services are our most critically important jobs? Why shouldn't this type of women's work be paid as well as, say, an investment banker, a plumber or a professor?

Conversations with younger feminists got me thinking about the ongoing inequities women continue to face in the workforce. How come one of my gal pals gets paid $70 an hour to perform at private kids' parties, face-painting and twisting balloon animals, while another gets paid $25 an hour to support ten adults with intellectual disabilities?

What if there was no such thing as 'women's work', just secure jobs with equal wages? These are some of the many questions that occupy my thoughts and leave me scratching my head. All I know is that if men were treated as unfairly as women at work, they would vacate boardrooms, down their tools, walk out of their sheds and take to the streets in protest.

While there has been some change, especially for women in professions and leadership positions, the rest of us plebs are stuck with unequal pay and worsening working conditions, clinging to low-paid jobs and hoping that the boss doesn't notice our working-poor despair.

If women are to create lasting change, we need much more than football teams, corporate leadership and one woman in power. Waiting for more women to climb the ladder and lead us all to glory will take forever. We need an inclusive feminist uprising. We need to be the bosses of our work and our lives.

Across four decades of working in offices, I have been amazed by the shifts in labour markets. The pace of technological change is head-spinning.

Back in the 1970s when I started work as a Girl Friday on reception, I used a twelve-line plug and cord switchboard, receiving an electric shock one day when I accidentally touched a cord to my lip. Then the office switched to a snazzy twelve-line press-button, dial-up landline phone. Then they introduced a desk-sized telex machine. Then a fax machine, which I turned off each night to save power until the boss found out and flipped his wig.

Then there was the new Café Bar machine. I would no longer have to collect and wash cups and take orders to make tea and coffee for the Jaguar car company staff, including the mechanics in the workshop out the back. But old roles die hard, and my dickhead boss made me make all the coffees and teas to order and hand them out on a tray. In the end I refused to play waitress and showed everyone how to self-serve, which was the whole point of the new brew machine. The blokes weren't happy, but I was.

Now we are completely online, lured by the promise of more leisure time. We fed the hungry beast of consumer capitalism, posting flawless photos and endorsing products and businesses as a side-hustle earn. We reimagined ourselves as social media influencers, and got paid to eat and wear stuff whether we liked it or not. Tethered to hotspots via handheld devices and smartphones, we got hooked on gazing at curated screen images of each other's lives. We bought more stuff online than we could ever use. Algorithms reinforced and redirected our choices, manipulating our free will, and gave voice to everyone all at once.

In this hectic, noisy, web-driven world, another great disruption to working life as I knew it surged: the gig economy. I first noticed an increasing number of motor scooter riders with branded backpacks zip around the streets. Soon, there were more riders in local cafes to collect food delivery orders than there were seated customers. It seemed odd to me that working people didn't have time to shop for food. But of course, workers were now on call to work 24/7. Let someone else worry about making your dinner, and get it delivered to your door. My unemployed mate spent her last $10 on a delivery of hot chips from her favourite hamburger shop, just around the corner, because what else could she get for ten bucks, and it made her feel special. Then I heard from number one sister that her well-off retired friends ordered a high-end feast from a posh Italian restaurant based in Melbourne, to be delivered to their holiday house 257 kilometres away. Some people have more money than sense – they'd need to microwave the food anyway.

News stories began to appear about food delivery drivers who were not exactly employees, but classed as independent contractors. They were not covered by insurance, were paid a pittance per delivery, and worked excessive hours. Sadly, some riders died on busy roads in their race to earn a living. The gig economy marked the beginning of a fractured, overwhelmed workforce. A rat race between regular wage earners and gig workers. The time-poor versus the job-poor.

During my ongoing unemployment, I noticed web adverts for online task services. A register for freelance help wanted. Everything from admin, to wheeling your bin out on rubbish night, packing up and moving house, cleaning and child care. An estimated low, flat-rate fee was calculated by the taskee. The tasker made contact, agreed to the rate, covered on-costs and travel to accept the task. All arranged via a brightly coloured website with fun graphics of people getting through their to-do lists.

This web-based service broke down jobs into tasks. Jobs that, in the past, would have been covered by an award hourly rate with superannuation, through a registered company employing and insuring staff on their payroll. Hosted via some of the biggest multinational corporations, these independent task contractors were on call at whatever pay rate was offered. The labour force that once built furniture evaporated. Instead, customers hired cheap-as-chips help to wrestle cheap-as-chips flat-pack furniture into shape with an allen key.

One day while I searched online for a massage therapist to ease my computer-based neck ache, I came across an awful web review posted by an anonymous woman. She had been waiting at a tram stop and walked into a nearby shop to ask about the tram timetable. When the receptionist of the massage centre did not know what the woman was talking about, the non-customer gave the business a no-stars rating, slagging off the 'dumb receptionist' on their business web page. Loony, entitled consumers roaming the streets offline and posting crazy online complaints against workers for every random interaction gone wrong. So much for the brave new world of interconnectedness.

Global financial meltdowns became regular events, and the social and economic fallout impacted workers' lives for years. Using our taxes to bail out failing banks, and allowing tax evasion by multinational corporations, we watched governments join the throng and go uber-corporate too. Out-of-control economic growth had caused an unhealthy, unstable environment and held a desperate workforce captive. Twenty-first century capitalism became the boss, and he was a destructive, demanding tyrant.

By early 2020, as global unemployment was reaching its highest level since The Great Depression, a total rearrangement of society and work had happened. Then the world changed dramatically again as the global coronavirus pandemic took over and put everything we knew on hold. Businesses went belly up, jobs were lost, housing and living costs soared, and unemployment and underemployment became the norm. Remote workers logged in and hung on to their livelihoods, working from home as lockdowns kept us all inside. Essential workers were hero-worshipped, saving lives at great cost to their own. Connected online to the workplace and disconnected from our social lives, we adapted to stay alive, and went back to the basics.

For working women, the world shrank and private and public worlds collided. The dream of working from home became a recurring nightmare of muted Zoom meetings competing with kids' demands for vegemite sandwiches, improvised home schooling, and housework on the run. Forget about lifestyle choices and work-life balance.

Meanwhile, wage theft was running wild, especially across tutoring, admin, retail and services sectors. It was every worker pit against the other in a battle of working longer hours for less pay. Interns signed up for work experience to join a merry-go-round ride of working for nothing; for 'exposure', for 'experience', and just to get a reference for their next unpaid gig. Older workers quit in droves. Workers across the world were paralysed with the fear of losing their livelihood. Excessive hours and job insecurity meant workers were too busy hanging onto their incomes to organise and agitate for change. Workers were afraid to join trade unions.

According to Jeremy Rifkin's 2000 book, *The End of Work*, at the dawn of a post-market era, there will be a new social contract. 'After centuries of defining human worth in strictly "productive" terms, the wholesale replacement of human labour leaves the mass worker without self-definition or societal function.' I know the feeling.

Rifkin counts on something called 'empowering the third sector'. He thinks community organisations, volunteers and the not-for-profit sector, supported by the government, will keep unemployed people busy supporting community services. The epitome of self-service.

Rifkin mentions female workers in his book only to say that, 'Many of the new part-time jobs are found in the so-called pink-collar ghetto – work concentrated in service and white-collar areas, such as secretaries, cashiers and waitresses that are occupied largely by women. But even many of these low-paying jobs are likely to vanish in the next decade.' In other words, women workers in future are going to be job-fucked.

How do we tame capitalism? Not on our own, that's for sure. United workforces hold the key. Strikes still wield power and withdrawing our labour is all we have left to bargain with. We have in the past demanded businesses and governments invest in communities, sustainable jobs, affordable housing, social welfare, public health care and education for everyone. Back in the day, workers protected the environment, fought for social justice and human rights – and we won.

We must again demand more humanistic ways of doing business and insist that governments be run for the people. We must stop crashing through this world and put the planet and people before profits. Because relocating to Mars is not an option, no matter how many lunatic billionaires insist otherwise as they rocket into space. The scientists reckon when you land on Mars you've got about eight minutes. That's a hell of a long way to go to die.

Following the devastating Australian bushfires during the incinerator summer of 2019 and 2020, I left the community radio station after seven years of volunteering on reception. I was keen to spend my time supporting more pressing environmental causes. I was also keen to get off reception and volunteer as a writer.

I was seventeen when I first volunteered with Friends of the Earth at the height of the anti-nuclear era. Forty-three years later, I rejoined collectives of environmentally friendly punks, eco-feminists and activists, fighting to protect the planet and working towards social and economic justice. Back at Friends of the Earth, I connected with people committed to recreating the world beyond rampant patriarchal capitalism. Right up my alley. I wasn't just an old Girl Friday anymore. I became an Eco-Feminist Marxist Humanist activist! Leaving work had also reignited that spark of rebellion that burned bright when I was a young, punk agitator. As an old, punk radical retiree, I had no bosses to answer to and no job to lose.

I produce their email newsletter, and research and write articles on fossil fuel expansion, and why it's such a bad idea during a climate crisis. I am supported, trained and encouraged to learn new systems and skills. Collaborating with staff and volunteers, young and old, we work at the grass-roots level on environmental campaigns, and it is my non-hierarchical dream come true.

Our organising structure, inspired by the murmuration of starlings, offers safety in numbers as we keep each other in flight. Thousands of activist birds swirling and swooping together, in balls of movement across the skies. Our Melbourne murmuration was made up of smaller groups of seven, with broader decision-making based on consensus. Our international efforts reach across the world. It is the antithesis of any workplace I have known and it took me time to adjust. At first, I was like a caged bird flying the coop.

Returning to the environmental movement after so many years was a continuation of my youth. It made me feel like I still had something to offer. That there was a real chance that if we worked together, we could save Mother Earth from profit-driven oblivion.

In early 2020, with global economic downturns lingering and looming, and the impacts of climate change rising, we united on the streets: students, unionists, old activists and young adults, demanding industry and government pull their fingers out. As the placards at mass global protests warned, 'There are no jobs on a dead planet.'

CHAPTER 10

Authoress in seventh heaven

AFTER I STOPPED full-time work, I felt a growing need to tell stories. While working full-time, I had limited mental capacity to write. I compromised my creativity for the need to earn money. I'd almost forgotten about my dream of becoming an authoress. It was only when I stopped working that I revisited notes from writing workshops that I'd done to kickstart my stories one day. Instead of itching, I scratched the surface of my life and let my story rip. Stories are my way of facing the past, letting out laughter and venting rage. My time feels more valuable when it's spent writing out the worries of the world. To be fully self-expressed is liberating.

What did I have to say? Well, I had spent more time at work than anywhere else, and I had some stories to tell. There was no longer any need to keep up with the hectic, changing working world. Instead, I observed it, thought about it and wrote about it.

As I explored the writing world, I noticed that working women's stories were mainly told through interviews and oral histories written by someone else. I really wanted to read stories written by working women, just so I could say, see? It's not just me.

Out and about, I often check out bookshops, the latest titles, always searching for stories by working women. Could I see my book sitting there one day?

One day I noticed there are a hell of a lot of rule books for life on the shelves, aimed mainly at women and written by 'experts'. Self-help books informing us that social and economic issues are our personal problem, that it's up to each individual to fix ourselves. That we'd get better by working hard, by being our best self, and by dreaming big. What a load of rubbish! How would anyone know how anyone else ought to live or work? All I know is that when I leaned into a work problem, they threatened me with the sack. When I pushed back, they sacked me. On my own, I was easy pickings, I was a problem employee to be dealt with, and no-one blinked an eye.

These rule books are just more reminders that the world thinks women are fundamentally flawed. That we need to be corrected, that we need to find our cure. That we need detoxing. That we need repairs like broken dolls. That women are problematic, we need help, and that there is always room for improvement, usually via consumption of bullshit products or flaky advice. Removed from the working world, I realised that I am fine just as I am. I didn't need or want continuous improvement. It's way too late for that anyway. Older, wider, wiser, funnier and freer, these wrinkly years are for me to be my true untamed self. Liberation from work was my reward.

As my post-work identity began to take shape, so did my stories. I really wanted to write out my working life story, but it was a long one and I didn't have a clue where to start. So, I looked over my short stories. They were always about two subjects: my childhood and my working life. I saw that they had the makings of book chapters. But I still didn't know how to write a whole book. Then I attended a weekend workshop on writing memoir and I found my form. I still had to convince myself that a working woman's story was worth writing, and that my story was worth reading. The generous memoir teacher told me to write it anyway.

Across a few years, I knocked out a first rough draft of about 20,000 words. Then my notebook computer died. Luckily, I had printed out a copy. My old-school admin habit meant I could retype and rewrite my story from hard copy onto my new laptop, and I kept a USB backup. I used hundreds of Post-it notes stolen from various office jobs to jot down my thoughts. Slowly and steadily my story – and the story of working women – unfolded.

In 2019 I attended another writing workshop about finding your voice. I ticked a tiny box down the bottom of the feedback form indicating that I was interested in finding a mentor from the Australian Writers Mentoring Program. I didn't think any more about it until I received an email a few months later. Someone had dropped out and would I be interested in being mentored by an award-winning author? I said yes and sent off a story outline and some money.

Once I had a mentor, I was away, crafting chapters to deadlines, and making meetings to discuss the drafts. Writing became my wonderful distraction, keeping my thoughts focused and my hands busy. While I had a very limited amount of money, I had plenty of time to write. Writing gobbled up an excessive amount of spare time. It was like having a job again.

I polished up my old short stories and some of them were published online by the ABC. One story made it into a literary journal that was catalogued into the collection at my local library. Then I was invited to write an article on women and work for the ABC TV program, *The Drum*. That 'one day' of becoming a writer had arrived.

I started to submit some of my short stories to select non-fiction prizes with themes, deadlines and no entry fees. This kept my writing going, and minimised rejections. For seven years, I scribbled notes, wrote short stories and then turned them into chapters. I kept attending writing workshops and festivals in the hope that, one day, it would all add up to a manuscript.

In early 2019 I was evicted from the Northcote flat after twenty-one years. The miserly landlord, who would perv through the windows and let himself in without permission to rifle through drawers, had finally decided to renovate the block of eight run-down flats. My eviction started because of a huge potted flowering succulent I'd had growing on the balcony for years. The landlords, second and third generation, told me to remove everything so they could paint the cement balcony black. The pot plant was way too heavy for me to move and I told them I couldn't shift it without help. They gave me an eviction notice.

Then they offered me one of the empty renovated flats next door for $400 a week. The putty-filled walls had been painted undercoat white, brown lino covered rough concrete floors, no new fittings, no laundry, and no heating or cooling. I politely declined their dud offer.

Instead, I landed an amazing near-new inner-city one-bedroom apartment by the river for $350 a week. My flawless twenty-one-year rental history put me in good stead with the new real estate agent and anonymous owners. It was safe and warm. It had a security system, heating and air con, my own euro laundry, was close to shops and transport, and even had an indoor swimming pool downstairs. The energy bills were half what I had coughed up living in the old hot-cold flat. I now had a wonderful space to live and to write without the aggravation of disrepair and the worry of escalating rent. My fears of homelessness, which had kept me in that dumpy old flat for so long, dissolved. I relocated to seventh-floor apartment heaven.

After Mum died, my sisters sorted her estate and to our surprise Laurel had somehow managed to leave each of her seven offspring a small inheritance. I spent mine on a few thousand dollars of dental work, moving costs and a lease on my new apartment. I also paid for the six-month writing mentorship.

During 2020, throughout Melbourne's rolling pandemic lockdowns, my mentor kept me writing, rewriting and opening up to lay my story bare, without fear. When we weren't in lockdown, we would catch up at a local cafe to discuss my chapters over coffee, or over Zoom. She carefully wore down my resistance, asking me to push the writing further, always spurring me on to dig deep into the past. She even encouraged me to be a bitch on the page as needed, which came naturally to me.

One of the best things about being the boss of my later life was that I made the rules. It was the first time in my life that I could take complete control over the way I wanted to live. After eight years out of work, at last it felt like I was on a lovely, long holiday at home. I had landed on my feet and had time to put it into words. Once I got the hang of it, writing and living off the clock was deeply satisfying. Writing made hours disappear. Weeks flew by and months flipped over like an old Hollywood movie calendar.

After forty years at work, what I bought was time. Work had taken most of my energy and many of my years, and now all I wanted was free time. Freedom to eat when I'm hungry, sleep when I'm tired, and speak when I want to. We sell our time for money, and we trade our time for a life worth living.

'Time is everything, man [woman] is nothing: he [she] is at the most time's carcass,' said Karl Marx. Women's time is also crowded with the needs of others. It is only when we are off the clock, away from the demands of work, free from family responsibilities, that we can fully live time as our own. As a philosophical carcass of time, I started living in a dream-like state, exploring a later life rich with imagination and contemplation, filled with possibility and free of obligations (apart from Centrelink).

Off the clock, time is endless. It's the complete opposite of watching time drag you down at work. Ploughing through the first three hours before lunch, then a quick coffee, a toilet break, then scoff down a sandwich. Tear through afternoon tasks, blurry-eyed from hours on a screen. Endless phone calls, messages and scheduling, rescheduling and corridor chit-chat. Being reminded that constant interruptions are the job. Long, boring meetings, taking minutes, saying nothing and making nothing happen. Staying late to finish that report. Home too late for dinner, toast, then toast again the next morning, to do it all over again. That was no way to live.

Getting up early had always gone against my body clock. Racing against time to clean, dress and feed myself before bolting out the door for the tram was sometimes hazardous. One workday morning, half asleep in auto-mode, I prepared a glass plunger of ground coffee and filled it with boiling water. In a hurry, I forced the clogged plunger down hard and it exploded over my chest, leaving a deep burn on my right tit. After cleaning the wound and wrapping ice cubes in a hanky to shove down my bra, I changed my top and headed to the office. For better or worse, for richer, for poorer, in sickness and in health, I went to work.

Now my mornings are spent in revolutionary contemplation, lying in bed checking emails, trawling daily news, reading stories and seeing where the day will take me. A leisurely shower and daily yoga salutes to the sun. A slow brunch of toast, juice, vitamin D tablet and two coffees. Washed dishes dried on a fancy granite benchtop. Thoughts about a late lunch and dinner as I walk by the river and nip over to the shops.

Out of work, there is time to buy food cheaply, and to eat what I want when I please. I have time to wait for the butter to soften, no need for manufactured margarine. Spreading the salty, creamy high-cholesterol richness to toast corners, golden melted pools scraped with yeasty vegemite or chunky apricot jam. Some days I'll have a lingering brunch of French raisin toast sprinkled with Dutch cinnamon, drizzled with Canadian maple syrup. Taking time to consider global trade. The maple tree sap tapped and bottled by workers across the other side of the world, wondering if they are sick to death of tapping the syrup, and if Dutch spice workers love their cinnamon as much as I do.

Zooming into book launches and online writing workshops, my little world at home has expanded. There is time to study the news, to read articles and books, to go to the shops, to do the washing, and to see family and friends. To have fun doing nothing much at all, and to feel no guilt for wasting my time. Not knowing the date if I don't need to. It is sheer relief to be in low demand. I have time to learn martial arts, and to go to the dentist. Before I knew it, I was too busy living to go to work.

Afternoons spent writing in my lounge room-kitchen, classical music on the radio, thinking about next story steps, forwards and back, dancing around my memories and my lovely new apartment. I discovered that late afternoons and early evenings were my favourite hours to write. It's knock-off time for workers. People re-emerge, carrying bags of food, collecting squealing children, hanging on hands to cross the road. The working world in relief, winding down and heading home to real lives.

High on my balcony I see blocks of urban-village skyline, a chimney stack puffing as I smoke a cigarette. A cartoon-blue sky and rose-gold sun sets behind the high-rises, a twinkling evening star in the west. The northern horizon is edged by river-gum tree tops; cranes and steeples poke through the leafy canopy, and I see mauve mountain humps in the distance.

As the city hum softens into nightfall, bats flap into the darkness, and birds fly home to their nests. Most nest-building birds are females, they do most of the construction. The female also chooses and maintains good nest sites for breeding. Some birds build special dormitory nests that are used only for roosting. From my seventh-floor apartment, I watch swallows circle and dive into the shelter of the underground car park, where they stick rows of conical nests onto solid concrete walls. These birds are apartment dwellers, and, like me, they've adapted to city life.

The swallows remind me of Will. We scattered his ashes off a country bridge on his birthday. Out of nowhere, from beneath the bridge, a gulp of swallows took flight through his floating particles, tearing away up the river. When we scattered Laurel's ashes on her birthday in the upside-down river near my new place, a duck darted across the muddy water, gobbled up her remains and paddled away. Life circles around us, and in the end, we are all bird droppings at the bottom of a river. Nourishing new life, feeding memories of love and loss in an endless cycle of regeneration, until we fly home.

Alone, I talk to a framed picture of Laurel. She is always with me. I talk to myself, working out my story. Sometimes chats on the phone with family and friends. Nights are spent streaming news, arguing with talking heads on the TV, laughing at comedies, watching a movie or bingeing a series. An easy dinner, fruit and yoghurt and medicinal dark chocolate for dessert. To bed whenever I like, to scroll social media and watch episodes of *Gogglebox*, watching people watching TV shows, simulating a shared viewing experience of long ago.

At this late stage and age, slowing down is a welcome relief. I bask in the luxury of timelessness, crowing and knowing that I worked hard for it. My liberation from white-collar labour is complete. My bed is a favourite place to think and re-think, knowing that I know nothing for sure. Except that as I age, everything will change again.

When I was a kid, as number six daughter I was always running up behind the pack of siblings singing out, 'Wait for me!' I was scared of missing out.

Some summers, we'd travel miles for a beach holiday with Aunty Valda and Uncle David and our cousins, staying at their South Gippsland dairy farm. We swam and played in the rock pools around Inverloch. On stinking hot days, we'd march single file to the bottom of the wild beach cliffs of Cape Paterson. I'd cling to Dad's slippery, red ears, perched high on his thick neck, my pudgy prep-school arm wrapped around his Germanic forehead. Little brother riding piggy-back slung against the lumbar of Dad's backache, gripping the tail ends of his flapping shirt. Five big sisters trailed behind descending the narrow, sandy track as the brutal sun bit our bare shoulders.

Mum was back on the farm, preferring to savour a Bex and a good lie down.

We'd tear through scrubby bush screaming across burning sand, 'the lava!' Blue plastic sandals cast adrift, we'd sink ankle-deep into the moving sandy shore. Spinning, laughing, we'd play scary sea monsters and frolicking dolphins in the wild waves, submerging and popping up to the surface, creating mermaid hairstyles and seaweed wigs. Sitting on the edge of the rock pools staring into miniature underwater worlds, we'd dream of a week of peace.

Huddled in the shade of a faded canvas green-and-gold striped beach umbrella spiked into the sand, five beach towels lay side by side as big sisters jostled for a tan. Us little kids waded in the frothy shallows, waves drawing us in and spitting us out. The big girls dived into the ocean swell. Eldest sister was on watch, warning me again not to go out any further. She pointed and read aloud from the rusty danger sign: 'Float with a current or undertow. Don't try to swim against it.'

Flipping underwater somersaults, diving into handstands, head held high movie-star swim-strokes, I was in way too deep. I couldn't touch the bottom, even on tippy toes. Breathing came before calling out. My body floated upright underwater, climbing an invisible ladder. Surfacing, a wave slapped me in the face. A monster rip grabbed my leg, pulling me down. Bubbles burst from my nose in a blur of churning sand and fizzy sea water. I gave in and went with the irresistible flow of the undertow.

Dappled yellow light danced on the sea floor. Pairs of feet attached to two liquid figures stood over me. Flapping, kicking horizontal on the sandy mound I lifted my sea-soaked head, blinking through saltwater eyes. The twin blurs looked down at what the sea had washed up. Two big sisters pulled me upright by my bather straps. Standing waist-deep in water on the outer sandbank, now I really was in trouble.

'What the bloody hell are you doing out this far, Krissy? You're not allowed on the sandbank!' growled second-eldest sister. Coughing, spluttering, I couldn't tell them the ocean pulled me under, how close it was. Big sisters flanked me in freestyle as I dog-paddled slowly back to shore.

I learnt early how to float on troubled waters, and how to resist the undertow. I counted on my big sisters, and they were always there looking out for me. But as the youngest daughter, I was a daredevil looking for the next risk to take.

One overcast day on the farm, I walked with the youngest siblings while the cousins rode their bikes up to the back paddocks.

'Hey Krissy, I dare you to ride down that big hill,' said one of the boy cousins.

'Okay, give me a lend of your bike and I'll show you,' I said, gripping the front wheel of his Dragstar between my knees.

I walked the bike to the top of the mighty slope and looked down to see the kids waving and yelling at me.

'Hey, I made it to the top!' I yelled, and waved back.

'Look behind you, behind you!' the kids shouted in unison.

I turned around to face the biggest black bull I'd ever seen, snorting and dragging his front hoof over the grass. I jumped on the bike and took off down the hill, gripping the handlebars as the fixed pedals whirled around, my feet flailing either side. Over rocks, tearing alongside the barbed-wire fence, I hit a ditch and went flying over the front wheel, skidding headfirst into the ground.

'That was the best thing ever, Krissy. You're Evel Knievel!' said the kids.

I checked for broken bones and slowly stood up, covered from head to toe in steaming bull shit. The kids bent over laughing, only straightening up to sing out, 'Pee-yeww!' before running back to the farm, busting to tell on me to Mum.

A wobbly dung monster, I staggered back to the farmhouse where Mum yelled, from a distance, to strip-off on the verandah while she ran a bath. As I undressed, I cried angry, triumphant tears. I had ruined my new jeans and striped jumper. But I had survived a spectacular, death-defying ride.

One mid-sixties summer day back at home, blistering sun scorched the terracotta rooftops as death reeked from the abattoirs half a mile away. Little brother and I tangled over rollerskates, trading insults through pinched noses. 'Ink pink you stink!' Hurtling down the intrepid hill of North Road, Clayton, flying over footpath cracks, coming a cropper on daisy patches, we'd check for broken bones and do it all again.

As Mum called us to come in for tea, our bruises and bloody scrapes were wiped with spit. Dying of thirst, starving hungry, skates removed because wheels were not allowed inside.

Mum's fried sausages and chips were on the way. We bagsed position, crammed together on the warm red brick front porch as grubby cotton-wool storm clouds splashed whopping drops above a distant rainbow. We dreamed of dessert.

'What's for sweets?' number two sister sang out to the kitchen.

'Ricky Nelson!' screamed number one sister from the lounge room, fixed on the black-and-white TV close-up of her teen idol dreamboat, and everyone laughed.

Dad had been away for about a week, probably met a mate up the milk bar, gone drinking and fishing we reckoned. Mum poured re-used golden oil into a pot on the stove to deep-fry chips. 'Buggered,' she muttered, going for a little lie-down. I went for a drink of water. Yellow flames crawled up the walls; the kitchen corner was ablaze.

'Mum, the kitchen is on fire!' I yelled.

'Go see if the old man is up the shed,' Mum screamed, 'Jesus, Mary and Joseph!'

Number five sister and I bolted up the backyard path. Glad to see he was home, we roared over the radio race caller.

'Dad the kitchen is on fire!'

'Righto love, righto,' he said, not looking up from the form guide. He thought we were kidding.

'No really Dad, the kitchen is on FIRE!'

He got it that time and ran to the house, ripped a wool blanket off a bed to smother the saucepan. He grabbed the handle over the blanket, ran out the back door and threw the flames hard across the long grass, beating the fire with pillows and leaving a black trail.

Mum started on the warpath but ended up shaking and sobbing, knowing the next fight must wait. Instead, she gave us comfort with baths and clean pyjamas then collapsed and fumed in her armchair as the kitchen corner smouldered. Our house stank of smoke, and shock shut us all up. We ate cold meat and salad, and the dishes were done in silence. Dad, puffed up with gingerly pride, returned to his shed. Us kids reckoned we were lucky he was home and sober.

Eldest sister disturbed the menacing quiet.

'So, who wants some Ricky Nelson?'

From that day on, the dessert with no name, leftover rice swimming in milk and crusted in sugar, was called 'Ricky Nelson'.

When I sent my siblings an earlier version of this story, testing the waters for their reactions, they said it took them straight back to the bad old days – except for number five sister, who insisted it was her who got Dad from the shed to put the fire out.

You know, honestly, I can't remember who was there, but I know our memories are parallel. Same family, different recall.

Recollecting forty years of work life has also been tricky. When I finished working, I made notes, venting my outrage onto the page to try to make sense of it, to let it go. But a lot of it made no sense, especially the last few years. Writing it out helped me to purge the past and to feel better about leaving the workforce behind.

My girlfriends helped me to clarify some of the most treasured and traumatic moments we shared at work. I couldn't recall much at all of the treatment and recovery years. I found out later that one of my close friends was more worried about me than I knew.

The funny moments were easy to recall, and the worst times were worse than we cared to remember. But as time rolled by, the sting of what had been so unfair at the time, eased. What seemed like monumental work problems that had kept me awake at night, and that I feared would haunt me forever, faded away, and I was left with the absurdity and hilarity of it all. What remained was an extraordinary story about an ordinary working life.

A few years back when I did have a job, I bought an orange and green paisley shirt at a groovy Smith Street clothes store. Before I wore the shirt, I checked the tiny tag on the inside seam for washing instructions.

Cold wash before wear
Dry in shade
Cool iron
Do not dry clean
80% cotton 20% polyester
Made in China
Fuck the insolation

For years I wore that shirt and showed people the tag with delight. The tag faded, then one day I finally understood that the anonymous factory worker had meant to say, *Fuck the isolation*.

During my working life, I was heartened by the mighty power of unions; the workers united, never defeated. The strikes and meetings when we joined together to put forward pay claims, health and safety and women's rights issues. Collective actions made us feel empowered and gave us the best chance for change. In standing up to the bosses together, we were not fighting each other, we were not fighting alone, and we were not suffering in isolation.

After I disconnected from the workforce, I felt excluded from the wider world. I realised I am on the outskirts of society. Whenever someone asked me, 'What do you do?' I'd say, 'Not much, how about you?' to find out who I was talking to so I could fit the conversation around their occupation. Sometimes I would say 'volunteer', which implied I had willingly left my career and now spent my idle time with other old ducks at a musty opportunity shop. Sometimes I would say 'I'm a writer', and bang on about my memoir, always a good conversation-stopper.

It was never easy saying 'retired' because that sounded like the end of the line for me. It was also what people with money chose to do. It was too much to explain to people that I had worked full-time for almost four decades, and that I had paid plenty of income tax. I didn't bother expanding on the democratic ideal of a government-funded social safety net for all. At first, I wouldn't admit to enjoying being out of the workforce. That would mean I was a dole bludger. This was the language neo-liberal governments and dodgy TV current affairs shows had used for so long. In other words, if you are out of work, you are a freeloader, a burden on working taxpayers.

When you don't have a paid job, blame and shame lands on you. You are told you are not pulling your weight. How dare you not work! You are less for not working, devalued, and rudderless.

It had to be my fault because if I really wanted to work, I would find a job. I would take any job, so they'd say. What alarmed me most was that my worth as a human being was measured mainly by my work. How hard I worked, how good I was at my job, and who I supported towards their career success. My workforce productivity counted for more than me. But I went to work all those years so I wouldn't have to go to work anymore.

Leaving work restored my mental and physical health. When I found a way out, partly by choice and partly by force, I gave myself the chance to live another life before it was too late. When I left work, I started living a life worth living.

My work had never felt like a career, more like a hard slog, day in day out for decades. When I added up all my jobs, I had a white-collar job path with a few too many career breaks into unemployment – the same as most workers. We are valued when we are in a job, and ignored when we are not.

Sometimes I heard manager colleagues talk about their work as their 'calling' and I wondered what they meant. I wasn't called to be an office chick. I just needed a job to bring home some money, and I could type. I didn't climb the career ladder because I was usually too busy hanging onto the job. I wasn't management material. Career-wise, I was just one of millions of minions who ought to count ourselves lucky to be in work supporting the aspirations of management.

I had no idea how I was going to support myself long-term, and that's still up in the air for me, and most working-class women. I asked myself, how much money would make me feel secure about my future? I realised that there would never be enough money. That financial security is fleeting, and it's a precarious reality I would learn to live with. If we hang on long enough, if we ward off sickness and sadness, if we secure paid work, if we have savings, we may get to enjoy the richness of post-work life. When the hormones die down and our limited energy is saved for the most important tasks ahead.

How quickly my youthful years flew by, and how precious time became now that the biggest chunk of my life was behind me. Time to look back on what was most important. I am certain it wasn't my work. It is people, those who I love and those who love me. As Karl Marx wisely said, 'Surround yourself with people who make you happy. People who make you laugh, who help you when you're in need. People who genuinely care. They are the ones worth keeping in your life. Everyone else is just passing through.'

When life slung the untimely cancer deaths of my dear friends Will and Mary at me, something shifted. I realised there weren't too many years left for me to muck around at the edges.

At sixty, I discovered the pure joy of my time being my own, to recollect and reflect, and to be okay with it all. This is my success in life. I made it this far through hard work and gritty determination. I crammed the good times into my life, and got through the hard times.

Life has given me a tough hide. It's pushed me off-course through unemployment, addiction, homelessness and illness. Life is like that: unfair, unmanageable and unknowable. As wounds healed, my skin grew thicker and scars formed a protective outer layer, an armour, ready for any battle. Trouble found me, and

I faced it. As Laurel used to say when she'd introduce me, 'This is my number six daughter, Kristine. She had a bit of trouble, but she's alright now.'

Looking back at my bread-and-butter earning years, it wasn't all bad. Supporting the transformative power of education, helping to alleviate the causes of poverty, telling people how to roast a turkey – overall, it was worth it. I worked hard to support myself and to contribute something of worth to the world. I learnt that we all need to feel valued and respected. And that it could all turn to shit again at any moment, so make the most of what you've got. Find out who you really are under that worker cloak, and indulge your passions like it's your last chance to dance. Life is a death-defying ride, so hang on tight, and pedal like a madwoman!

When I stopped work, I found out who I really was. I am a punk, a comedian, a writer, a caregiver, an aunty and a friend. I am a freedom fighter, a unionist, a feminist activist and an environmentalist. When I stopped work, I renewed my relationships with people I love, who mean much more to me than work. I also mourned the years I spent in jobs that I hated. I discovered that I am worth much more to the world than my labour. That my time is worth more to me than money. That the worth of my work is not the worth of me.

I also found out that it takes a lot more courage to live life than it does to write about it.

It took sixty years of living, forty years of working and ten years of writing to tell my story. Maybe it will inspire readers to write, to join a trade union, to stick up for themselves and for each other at work, to find the right job or to leave the wrong one. To spend their later years however they please.

Working all those years allowed me time to write in later life. I had finished the nine-to-five slog and I had plenty of tales to tell. Which worked out fine, because if this story is ever published, I'll never work in this town again.

My family and friends, my smarts, stories and work got me through. I discovered along the way that I did want more than a job and a home. It was only after I stopped work that I realised what I truly wanted, more than anything else: to become a writer, to share my stories created in a warm, safe place. And I want working women's stories to matter.

No doubt there will be more trials to overcome. But I am not waiting for my life to begin. I am not scared of missing out on anything. I just want to stick around to see how my story ends.

THE END

Acknowledgements

To my friends, family and fine colleagues, to my writing mentor Carrie Tiffany, and to Emily Hart, Elena Callcott and Pam Brewster from Hardie Grant. I couldn't have lived this life and told my story without you all in it. Thank you from the bottom of my heart.

I write and live on the land of the Wurundjeri People and I acknowledge that sovereignty of the lands of the Kulin Nation were never ceded. I pay respect to First Nations elders, past, present and emerging.

About the author

Kristine Philipp began life in Melbourne in 1960. In 1975 she started office work, on and off for forty years, in the university sector, small business, the public service and community organisations. In 1984, she was the subject of a half-hour episode for *Faces of Change*, an ABC TV documentary series and book about women in Australia, and was remembered by Anne Deveson in her 2003 book *Resilience*. Kristine inspired and helped to develop the lead character in Mary Callaghan's 1988 feature film *Tender Hooks*. She won a scholarship and graduated with BA Hons in cinema-media studies in 2000. Kristine has written and performed stand-up comedy shows at Fringe Festivals, and writes articles for Friends of the Earth. Kristine's creative non-fiction short stories are published in a local literary journal, on ABC online and are produced as audio stories. Kristine is an unemployable old punk, and *Girl Friday* is the memoir of her working life.